FREE-HEEL SKIING

Telemark and Parallel Techniques
for all conditions

FREE-HEEL SKIING
Telemark and Parallel Techniques for all conditions

THIRD EDITION

Paul Parker

Foreword by Yvon Chouinard

BÂTON WICKS

~*To Liz.*~

Published in Great Britain by Bâton Wicks Publications, London. All trade inquiries U.K. and Commonwealth (except Canada) to: Cordee, 3a DeMontfort Street, Leicester, England, LE1 7HD

Published by The Mountaineers Books
1001 SW Klickitat Way, Suite 201, Seattle, WA 98134

© 1988, 1995, 2001 by Paul Parker

All rights reserved

Third edition, 2001

No part of this book may be reproduced in any form, or by any electronic, mechanical, or other means, without permission in writing from the publisher.

Manufactured in the United States of America

Project Editor: Julie Van Pelt
Copy Editor: Linda Robinson
Production Coordinator: Dottie Martin
Cover Design: The Mountaineers Books
Book Designer and Layout Artist: Jennifer LaRock Shontz
Illustrator: Steve McDonald
Photographers: Scott Cramer, Ace Kvale, Brian Litz, John Norris (www. chamonixart.com), Paul Parker, and Mark Shapiro

Front cover photograph: *Erik Assum in Chamonix, France.* © John Norris
Back cover photograph: *Robert "Bernie" Bernthal on Grand Combin, Verbier, Switzerland.* © Mark Shapiro
Frontispiece: *The author in his preferred element. The Battle Range, British Columbia, Canada.* © Brian Litz

Library of Congress Cataloging-in-Publication Data
Parker, Paul, 1953-
  Free-heel skiing : telemark and parallel techniques for all conditions
/ by Paul Parker ; [illustrator, Steve McDonald].— 3rd ed.
    p. cm.
Includes bibliographical references (p.) and index.
  ISBN 0-89886-775-4
  1. Telemark (Skiing) 2. Telemark (Skiing)—History. I. Title.
  GV854.9.T44 P37 2001
  796.93—dc21
                                    2001002408

British Library Cataloguing in Publication Data
A catalogue record for this book is available at the British Library.
ISBN 1-898573-54-9 (U.K.)

♲ Printed on recycled paper

Contents

Foreword

Until I started watching and listening to Paul Parker, I had pretty much taught myself to ski by just going out and doing it. I have short, strong legs and had done enough backcountry skiing to get pretty good at survival turns.

I was introduced to cross-country skis and the telemark turn many years ago by Doug Robinson and his band of "Armadillos" on the east side of the Sierra. At the time, I couldn't understand why they insisted on messing with the pine tar and klister and zigzagging around instead of simply slapping on some skins and going straight up the hill. And those weird drop-knee turns! Why not just parallel or do survival stem christies?

A few years later I found myself coming down Denali pulling a 50-pound sled through 18 inches of heavy new snow. I put the load on my back, thinking I could easily ski this stuff on my alpine touring skis, but soon realized that with the load, the wet snow, and the floppy mountain boots there was no way I could begin to initiate a turn. So I unlatched my heels and headed down with a sort of snowplow/stem/telemark/steering turn. No unweighting was necessary or possible. This experience was a revelation to me and soon afterwards I hung up my fat boards and went skinny.

Corn was the new diet. A typical morning in May or June might find me hiking up some slope in the Tetons or Absarokas, maybe sitting on top for an hour or so to let the corn become velvet, then cutting down in wide, classic telemarks.

But it was while skiing with Artie Burrows, Julie Neils, and Murray Cunningham in Aspen that my eyes were first opened to the full potential of skinny skis. Not only were these people outskiing nearly everyone on the mountain regardless of gear, but theirs was not the Peruvian-hat, double-poling, Al Jolson-mammy-turn technique I had known. These jaded ex-alpine racers were blending the old with the new to create an entirely original sport.

Photo on preceding page
© Mark Shapiro

I was stoked, but I had some work to do! This is about the time I started to really watch and listen to Paul Parker.

Paul is my kind of instructor. He gives me a one-sentence technique tip, then leaves me alone until he sees that I've digested it. I have been given more than a few tips by him over the years while skiing *toute neige-toute terrain* in various off-beat parts of the world as we've traveled together testing equipment.

There was a day in Steamboat, skiing hardpack, paralleling the steep stuff, and telemarking the intermediate hills. I'd always had trouble with my left-hand teles and Paul told me to think about pressing the little toe of my back foot against the slope. This worked to get my feet closer together and my skis on edge and corrected my habit of going into my left turns from a stem.

A few days later, a foot of heavy, skied-out cement in Breckenridge stopped me cold. Paul told me to exaggerate my ups and downs the way skiers used to do before high-top plastic boots. This worked, too.

In Hokkaido we met up with fifteen members of the 200-member Japanese Telemark Association. None of them had skied outside Japan, and they were anxious to watch Parker to see if they were on the right track. They were all excellent skiers on the pistes, skiing in perfect Austrian feet-locked-together style. No yelling, and no smiling. When it snowed a meter we headed for the trees—all birch and giant bamboo—and Paul gave me a powder tip. He told me to pretend to grip a pencil between my hip and waist. This got my skis off to the side and together. Switching from side to side got the powder rhythm going and I made five or six good turns before I blew it. Not bad, though. Nor were the Japanese much better in the powder. I sensed them wondering why we didn't just go back to those nicely packed slopes.

The next day Paul told me not to let my hand drop down and back. As soon as I planted my pole, the other hand came forward. "Let out a big, aggressive grunt every time you do a turn," he said. I did this and suddenly it all came together—we were like two hooting kamikazes, grunting and screaming through the trees, finally breaking out of the woods and laughing our heads off, covered from head to toe in the white stuff. Very un-Japanese.

I can't always listen to Parker. Sometimes I have to just watch. A few years ago several of us spent a week in the Sierra skiing the peaks north of Mount Whitney. It was late spring and there had been a day of wet snow and rain followed by a couple of cold nights, so when going out over Sheppard's Pass it was no surprise to find the north side a sheet of ice. No way was I going to even attempt traverses or kick turns on that 35 degrees of smooth ice. I climbed down the rocks, paralleling the gully as far as I could, and searched through my pack for something sharp and hard to scratch steps when I looked up to see Parker with his 40-pound pack jump-turning down in perfect control. We all watched fairly aghast, when Paul stopped, looked down at his feet, and calmly announced that the bail on one of his experimental bindings had broken on one side. He pushed off again, this time being careful to keep the one ski on the ice so he didn't jump out of the binding. By the time he was safely down I was so shattered that I threw off my heavy pack and watched it whirl down in great leaps for hundreds of feet to the snowfield below. Then I pulled out a couple of tent pegs and started scratching nicks in the ice, lowering myself down on my belly.

"Hey, Paul. Wait for me."

— Yvon Chouinard

Preface

Over thirty years ago, telemark skiing began a slow rebirth in the United States. When this rebirth started, few young skiers knew about telemark, and many older skiers didn't care to remember it. It was a technique that our parents and grandparents had used before ski lifts, the Arlberg technique, and alpine bindings.

This early wave of telemark skiing started in America's heyday of alpine skiing—Hexcel Sundances; red, white, and blue sweaters; jet sticks; and painful black Langes. The expense, the distasteful, flashy style, and the physical discomfort of alpine skiing—especially painful boots—were good reasons to pursue telemark. But we really didn't need good reasons. Telemark was a beautiful, graceful, functional turn. It felt pure; it was a secret unknown to the masses. The gear was inexpensive, comfortable, and lightweight—even if it didn't afford much control.

Telemark skiing was countercultural. It was a response to the flash of the alpine scene. Telemarkers were usually younger, backcountry skier types, college students, dope smokers, mountaineers. That day's telemark gear gave us access to the backcountry.

Very few alpine skiers knew what telemark skiing was, so they ignored us. We didn't try to ride lifts much, so access wasn't a serious issue. But as tele skiers became more eager to make turns and less eager to climb for them, ski areas felt a need to restrict our access. So for a few years ski areas limited what terrain we could use. I remember trying to go helicopter skiing in the Canadian Bugaboos with my tele skis and being turned away by Canadian Mountain Holiday's guides.

Racing helped give telemark skiing some exposure and, eventually, acceptance at ski areas. Races were organized opportunities to dress up in old clothes, run a few gates, and, mostly, enjoy a three-day party.

But racing changed over time. Hotshots from all over the United States,

Photo on preceding page
© John Norris

and eventually from Scandinavia and Europe, congregated at big races. They got more and more serious, kept score, and organized what had once been chaotic and just for fun. It was the inevitable result of people's competitive drive to compare themselves with others. But, unlike what has happened in many other sports, racing didn't come to dominate telemark. A few people followed the racing scene religiously, but most chose not to. In the United States it's still all-round skiing on- and off-piste that drives the sport. The modern term is **freeriding.** That's what this book is about.

In those early days of telemark it was the mystery that kept it going. Today, we're just skiers like everyone else—the sport is accepted. But look around, and although you'll see more tele skiers than in the early days, somehow it still holds a bit of that mystery. We are in the minority. I like that.

This book is a culmination of thirty-odd years of free-heel skiing and teaching. That sounds like a long time, but when I went skiing for the first time this season, I was so excited that I couldn't sleep the night before. Skiing still does that for me. I hope it does that for you.

Throughout this book I've used the term **free-heel** with skis, skiers, and skiing. Free-heel is an inclusive term that also points to the most essential difference between skiers who use alpine and skiers who use "nordic" equipment. Backcountry, cross-country, and telemark skiers and equipment are free-heel. This book is written for those skiers, whether they're at the beginner, intermediate, or expert level.

How should you use the information in this book? If you are a beginner, pick the section that applies to you, and practice. Be patient—build a foundation. You need mileage. I've purposefully been spare in the language because in your case, mileage is more important than words. Look at the pictures. Work on only one tip at a time. Enjoy the process—don't be too hard on yourself.

Intermediate and advanced skiers need mileage, too; but we have to be sure that you don't complete that mileage with bad habits. Find the technique and level that apply to your skiing, and start there. Then, when you have some time, read back over the beginning sections.

Once I've moved through the early teaching progressions, most of the techniques in this book are refined through tips, or points of focus. Why? Because it's been my experience in both my own skiing and in teaching others that that's what works. A note of caution: think about these points one at a time—not several at once. I've given you a lot of them so that you get your money's worth, but remember that each tip deserves practice. They aren't meant to be crammed into too short a time. Take these tips one by one.

Think about goals, too. Each winter I set a goal for my skiing. That goal might be skiing a certain tour, a special race, or descending a peak or couloir I've been eyeing. Often my goal has been technique related—learning a new one, perfecting an old one, or ridding myself of a bad one. Of course, there's room for more than one goal, as long as I can see them all the way through. Goals keep me interested. They give me something to look forward to through the winter, and they give me something to work for.

It helps to set a goal, but you don't have to be overly intense about it. I like to set goals that are fun. Having a goal keeps you focused in your learning. Be patient. You've got time. One of the things that I love about skiing is that it's something that one doesn't grow out of.

This book was written for your enjoyment—to help you reach your skiing goals and to have fun in the process!

ACKNOWLEDGMENTS

With special thanks to Andrew Denton for his proper English feedback. And thanks to Erik Assum, Bernie Bernthal, Yvon Chouinard, Scott Cramer, John Dostal, Elizabeth Hutchins, Michael Kennedy, Ace Kvale, Brian Litz, Bob Mazarei, Steve McDonald, Roanne Miller, John Norris, Paul Peterson, Carl Scofield, Mark Shapiro, Lito Tejada-Flores, John Tidd, and Nanni Tua.

And to Allan Bard, and his memory.

Photo on following pages
© John Norris

BEGINNINGS

Free-heel's Roots

"The real fathers of the sport were not the men who made a few half-hearted experiments with skis and then abandoned the fickle boards in despair, but those who first proved by solid achievement the wonderful possibilities of the ski."

—Arnold Lunn

Throughout modern ski history one theme recurs: the gradual development of two separate skiing disciplines, alpine and nordic. Early masters of the two schools fought like rival siblings to establish theirs as the superior one. Yet neither style succumbed. Instead, each grew more specialized for its home terrain. Alpine developed sophisticated downhill maneuvers; nordic evolved for cross-country travel.

The rebirth of the telemark has brought these two rivals back onto the same terrain. Yet there is still a distance that separates the two, one that, fortunately for the sport of skiing, is shrinking. What today is only a technical or aesthetic difference began as a heartfelt rivalry a hundred years ago.

The feud between nordic and alpine came late in the sport's development, once ski technique had matured. Long before that, skiing had originated in the far north. Most historians credit Scandinavia with the birth of skiing; but some believe it was introduced in China, not as a means of travel across snow but to support people on peat bogs and mud flats while they collected duck eggs.

Historian Arnold Lunn supports this theory. "Pattens have been employed from time immemorial not only on snow, but for crossing mud, sand, lava. . . . " For most, however, skiing began on snow in Scandinavia.

Photo on preceding page
© Paul Parker

Numerous archaeological discoveries in Norway, Sweden, and Lapland substantiate this theory.

Early skis varied in length and shape and were made from ash, pine, or birch. Some were solid boards with the tips soaked or steamed and turned up. Others were frames of wood covered in leather. Skiers used one long pole, which they dragged as a brake and used as an outrigger. While many skis in the far north were short and wide, a pair of Lapland skis had two different lengths. The shorter ski had a kind of "climbing skin" made from fur for uphill purchase; the longer ski was used for glide. Farther south, skis were long, and the two skis in a pair were of equal length, resembling skis used in the 1930s.

THE NORWEGIAN TECHNIQUE

Sondre Norheim is considered the father of the Norwegian technique. It was Norheim who, in the late 1800s, developed the telemark on the slopes around his town of Morgedal in the Telemark region of Norway. He introduced the telemark to the world at a jumping competition in Oslo in 1868, where he not only awed a large crowd with his 76-foot jump but also punctuated his landing with a graceful telemark turn to a stop.

The telemark turn wasn't just a curiosity but a viable technique for the equipment of the day, which consisted of free heels and wooden skis with no sidecut. In the telemark position one could wedge the forward ski slightly and have the effect of one long, sidecut ski. When properly performed the result was an elegant arc, most often a medium-to-long-radius turn well suited to Norway's moderate terrain and deep snow.

Another significant contributor to this Norwegian school was the explorer Fridtjof Nansen. In 1888 Nansen completed a 500-kilometer journey across southern Greenland and in 1890 published a book about the expedition, *The First Crossing of Greenland*. It was the first widely read account of ski technique, development, and philosophy.

Inspired by the California Gold Rush, the Norwegians took their technique to America. Many emigrating Norwegians stopped en route to California and settled in the Midwest, but one, John A. Thorenson, made it all the way to California. Thorenson was later nicknamed "Snowshoe Thompson" for the mail route he pioneered over the formidable Sierra Nevada. For twenty years he carried mail from California to the Nevada mining camps. The combined weight of his oak skis and the mail on his back sometimes exceeded a hundred pounds.

THE ALPINE TECHNIQUE

Although later bolstered by nationalistic pride, the split between alpine and nordic skiing did have technical roots. The alpine countries of central Europe depended on ski troops for the defense of their mountainous borders. Yet negotiating the Alps, with their steep, unforgiving couloirs and rock-strewn slopes, required a different style of skiing. The alpine school evolved using braking techniques with smaller, more controlled turns.

The Austrian Mathias Zdarsky is most often credited as the father of alpine technique. In his book *Lilienfelder Skilauf Technik*, Zdarsky documented the snowplow turn he performed on his short, compact skis.

Father or not, it sounds as if Zdarsky must have been a real ass. He vehemently promoted the rift between the alpine and nordic schools and directed personal, vindictive abuse against his colleagues using Norwegian technique in the nearby Black Forest. In retrospect it is amusing. Arnold Lunn referred to the infamous feud as the "Battle of the Bindings."

The bindings were different, but unlike today's, both alpine and nordic bindings were free-heeled. The early nordic bindings resembled today's cable bindings in that they hinged farther back, under the ball of the foot. The alpine bindings, however, hinged in front of the toe, like a modern randonnée binding. It's no wonder that Zdarsky didn't like telemark turns: anyone who has tried to telemark on randonnée gear knows the desperate insecurity of tiptoeing on the rear foot.

Zdarsky skied with only one long pole. Georg Bilgeri, an Austrian colonel, popularized the use of two shorter poles. Bilgeri checked his speed with his turns, like a modern skier, unlike many monopole skiers who used their "ski stock" as an outrigger. He published his techniques but didn't follow any particular "school" of skiing. Bilgeri suggested that alpine skiers use the strong points of both the Norwegian and alpine schools, describing, for example, the *stembogen*, or stem turn—a snowplow turn linked by a diagonal run and inspired by both the snowplow and the telemark.

Zdarsky suffered sour grapes over any fame that Bilgeri might have enjoyed. He was so angered by Bilgeri's description of the *stembogen* in the book *Der Alpin Skilauf* that he challenged the colonel to a duel. Yes, a duel—with guns—over ski technique. Had the duel been carried out and had Bilgeri been a good shot, the modern relationship between nordic and alpine might be much different.

But Zdarsky wasn't the only one who fueled the split between the two techniques. Part of the handiwork belonged to Rudolph Lettner, an Austrian metalworker who put metal edges on his skis to keep them from splintering. Not only did the edges increase the life of his skis, but they gave his turns more carve and less skid.

Hannes Schneider, a student of Bilgeri's, was responsible for developing the so-called Arlberg technique, which used more commitment, more angles of the body. The Arlberg skier stood far forward with upper body rotated. The turns were initiated with a stem. Schneider developed the Arlberg as a system for alpine instruction. He combined telemark and *stembogen* into his Arlberg turn, an early version of the stem christy. He presented his progression of skills to ski schools in 1912, and it dominated downhill ski instruction worldwide until the 1940s.

Telemark was officially dead, at least for alpine instruction. The techniques split—Arlberg for downhill skiing, telemark for tourers in up-and-down terrain.

POSTWAR DEVELOPMENTS

The Second World War brought skiing as a sport to a standstill. Ironically, for Americans the war set the stage for skiing's future. Since fighting in the mountains of Europe necessitated skiing and mountaineering skills, Minot "Minnie" Dole—who later founded the National Ski Patrol—formed the Eighty-seventh Mountain Infantry Division. The Eighty-seventh was soon renamed to what it is known as today: the Tenth Mountain Division. After the war, surviving veterans of the Tenth Mountain Division returned to start the ski areas, ski schools, ski shops, and ski-manufacturing companies that have turned the sport of American skiing into a viable industry.

Nordic skiing did not see as much development, but alpine grew rapidly. In 1946, the first ski-snowshoe race was held at Arapahoe Basin in Colorado. First prize was a can of beer. In 1950, Aspen hosted a World Cup race. In that same year, Cubco bindings were introduced. Their spring-loaded heel piece held the ski-boot heel securely on the ski. This specialization in equipment set the modern course for alpine skiing as the lift-serviced sport that we know today. Free-heeled bindings remained popular with off-piste skiers and ski mountaineers, but for lift-serviced alpine skiers Cubcos became state-of-the-art.

As alpine skiing grew, many more ski lifts were built. Downhill skiers, confined to paths down resort slopes, soon formed moguls. The Arlberg became a dated technique. Its slow, elegant, exaggerated movements were incompatible with the bump-studded hills. Alpine turns became quicker.

In 1959, Cliff Taylor developed his Graduated Length Method (GLM), a mixed blessing in the development of skiing. Admittedly, it did allow more people to learn the sport more easily; but what had once been nice, round moguls developed into evil little ski-bending bumps. With the development of GLM, many alpine skiers, disgusted by hackers' short skis ruining even the steepest slopes, ventured into the backcountry.

In the early 1970s, in a number of little backcountry pockets around the snowy United States, skiers exhumed the telemark, a technique that brought downhill stability to their free-heeled gear. They could tour off the alpine trails and make sweeping turns in idyllic snow inaccessible to the short alpine skis. They could get back to the sport's beginnings, where many of them thought it should have stayed in the first place. Crested Butte, Colorado, was one of these little pockets where the telemark was reborn. That is where I was first exposed to it.

Rick Borkovek was an important contributor to telemark's rebirth. A long-time resident of Crested Butte who now resides in Aspen, Rick published a number of articles on the tele's comeback that inspired mountaineers and ski tourers to give it a try. Manufacturers were urged to make new products for telemarkers. First they developed plastic-laminated cross-country skis with aluminum edges. These evolved into "skinny alpine skis" with tunable steel edges. As skis got wider, boots got higher and stiffer, first home-modified by the hard-core piste skiers, then factory-made as the demand grew.

In the mid-1970s, the competitive urge and a need for recognition inspired an alpine-style racing series for telemarkers: the Summit Series. First it was just for fun; then it got serious. Racers were required to make telemarks and were penalized for any technical transgressions. Those interested in honing their parallel technique stayed out of the gates—or off the piste.

In 1980, the Professional Ski Instructors of America (PSIA) formed a demonstration team that, in 1983, introduced the modern American telemark and teaching methods to the world at Interski in Sesto, Val Pusteria, Italy. Telemark teaching grew at many ski areas, and the PSIA eventually offered a Nordic Downhill certification.

Free-heel skiing continues to grow. To mountaineers and backcountry skiers, telemarking satisfies the special appeal of doing more with less. It is a departure from the norm. It is a challenge. Most important, it is fun.

The Battle of the Bindings has come full circle. Alpine and nordic skiers now carve turns on the same terrain. Accomplished free-heel skiers are mastering alpine techniques. Less popular are the labels, the "schools."

As Fridtjof Nansen wrote, ". . . nothing steels the willpower and freshens the mind as skiing. This is something that develops not only the body but also the soul—it has far deeper meaning for a people than many are aware of. . . ."

Denali

~

It was a cold, drizzly morning on Denali's Muldrow Glacier. Although we had almost 24 hours of daylight, we were in a hurry to be off before the snow got too soft. Soon we would have to go on the night shift, moving in the evening when the sun's low arc left long, cold shadows on the snow's frozen surface.

Gearing up that morning was epic. It had been like that every day. It was too late to say it, but the problem was the array of equipment we had chosen. Most of the group had prototype randonnée bindings, and there lay the problem: the bindings still had bugs. When they worked perfectly they were better than our nordic setup because the stiffer boots and wider skis gave more control. But they never worked perfectly.

Two of us were using old double-Galibier touring boots, the only ones available in 1975. We had edged nordic skis and heavy steel cable bindings. Our equipment was simple—all we had to do was step in, bend over, and flip the front throw. We had none of the others' pre-releases, iced binding mechanisms, or hinges to grease. But our system was far from perfect.

High on the mountain, we left our skis behind. It was a good thing we had judged the boilerplate unskiable. The mountain was winning as, one by one, our mountaineering bindings fell apart. Our ugly-duckling nordic gear—nothing fancy, just simple and dependable—held fast. Still, I was relieved by the failures; I didn't want to ski those hard, exposed slopes on any of our gear.

I had expected that since my boots could flex, my feet would be warmer. I had no idea how cold that mountain really was; above 16,000 feet my boots remained frozen solid. I clumped along just like everybody else. We reached the summit in good weather, but it was still brutally cold. My feet were on the edge. I wiggled my toes unconsciously; I couldn't have stopped if I had wanted to. It was the one time I would have gone for a pair of those huge, goofy "mouse" boots. Summit time was brief; a few photos and we started squeaking down, crampons noisy in the cold névé.

The descent down the glacier was long—18 miles—and uneventful. We were so terrified of crevasses we used our skins when descending the lower slopes. Cracks were everywhere, creaking and groaning. Now it was too warm.

Our skis were like snowshoes. I began wondering why we had taken skis at all—because we just didn't know when to quit? Used just for transportation, they were unwieldy and undependable. But I wanted to make them work for mountaineering, to find the gear and adventures that were the ideal match. There was great room for improvement.

Free-heel Equipment

I work in product development for free-heel skiing. Every now and then I get comments from free-heel skiers about the new gear's technology: that big plastic buckle boots, fat skis, and cable bindings—much less the new step-ins—are too heavy, with too much control. That using them is "cheating." That somehow we've lost the soul of the sport.

For me, the sport's soul isn't about gear, it's about freedom. There is no such thing as cheating. No one is judging us; no one cares what we do. Telemark skiing is about rebellion: do what works for you and stay away from restrictive dogma like that which, years ago, we resisted in the alpine world. Tele is a sport like climbing that you do for yourself, not for the benefit of others. It's that freedom that I love about telemark.

Technique is even more controversial than technology. Simply by using the word **telemark** we imply that tele is the sport. Yet telemark is not the sport, it's just one of the turns. Some die-hard knee-droppers and traditionalists poo-poo the use of the alpine turn in the same vein that others poo-poo new gear. In both cases, it's usually because they don't have much experience with it. I say, try it all. Experiment. Do what gives you the most pleasure and satisfaction. That's what freedom is about.

In the old days, we said we tele-skied to reach mythical untouched powder slopes. But really we were making a statement—we chose an alternative to the exaggerated red-white-and-blue flash of then-booming alpine skiing. We distanced ourselves from alpine skiers, scorned lifts, got high, dressed differently, spouted vegetarianism.

The funny thing about this "statement" was that we were embarrassed to admit that we were downhill skiing, and liked it. Telemark was the object of too much fervent passion to admit that what had sucked us into the sport was something as banal as the simple thrill of gliding with gravity. If spotted on the piste, we always justified our presence apologetically: "Just practicing for the backcountry." Or "I skinned up."

Photo on preceding page
© John Norris

But telemark was reborn to go downhill. And downhill skiing, free-heeled or not, is about speed, finesse, grace, and control.

And—especially when conditions are challenging—it's about *leverage*. That's where technology comes in, the new stuff—big gear.

Technology is good. Technology rules—at least if it makes you ski better and have more fun. Sure, telemark has a tradition of doing more with less. We still do. That is one of its most attractive elements. Even with the heaviest of today's technologically advanced hardware you can tour. We are skiing better, steeper, faster with better technique, with less. We have the leverage to manage all conditions. We can ski the worst junk snow that nature leaves behind with grace and consistency.

Today's trend is touring to make turns. With this emphasis, skiers are choosing much sturdier gear for the backcountry. That doesn't mean that there isn't a choice, that one can't still get very lightweight gear for backcountry skiing. In fact, there are many more choices out there, heavier and lighter, and although many skiers choose the most control that they can find for the downhill ride, others choose high tech's lighter weight alternatives.

Make your own choice. If you don't like skiing on the heavier stuff, don't. If it spoils the soul of the sport for you, then don't put down your credit card for it. Choose the best kind of gear for the sort of skiing that you expect to do. You don't need to over-equip yourself. What's important is *skiing*—not the gear. Buckle down, get out there, rip it up, mix tele turns with some alpine turns. Experiment.

And don't be afraid to admit that you like downhill skiing!

This chapter describes the kind of free-heel gear designed for downhill performance, for the biggest grins when you're touring for turns, hiking for off-piste, and terrorizing the resort. To that I've added some favorite backcountry gear tips, because much of the best snow and terrain requires self-propelled access…those mythical untouched powder slopes.

SKIS

I like skis on the wide side—at least 70 millimeters underfoot. I find them especially effective in loose, variable snow in the backcountry. Wide skis ride higher in the snowpack, an advantage in heavy conditions when submarining skis get bogged down and hard to steer. Wider skis can be skied a little shorter. A shorter length makes them even more maneuverable when you need to use subtle rotational movements instead of big, sweeping moves—those that reap havoc with a pack. What length? Depending on the dimensions of the ski, I usually ski around 180–185. This length usually corresponds to a "medium" size in that ski model's range of lengths.

Shape

The **shape** achieved with what were once extremes in width and sidecut has had an enormous effect on ski performance. Add **flex** to that mix and—assuming good quality construction—you have what I consider to be a ski's most important design ingredients: **width, sidecut,** and **flex.** These ingredients are most easily described separately, but they don't act independently. They work together in synergy to determine a ski's performance—and more fun for the skier.

Width and sidecut. In 1861, Sondre Norheim began cutting a concave arch into the sides of his wooden skis. This arch formed a narrower mid-section, called the **waist,** with wider tips and tails. These skis were **sidecut.** By applying body weight to the edge of a sidecut ski, the waist of the ski presses down to contact the snow, forming a bend—an arc—in the ski (illus. 1).

Today, experimentation with extremes in sidecut has birthed a new generation of skis. Wide, solid, and stable, they have a new shape. When shopping for a new pair of skis, that is one of the first things that you'll ask, or the salesperson will offer—how much **shape** (sidecut) does the ski have?

Sidecut has its advantages, and when taken to an extreme, a few disadvantages. Its pluses, briefly, are easier turn initiation and better edge hold—more carve, less skid.

Its minuses are that too-shaped skis can be "hooky," nervous, with too much edge hold—especially when trying to exit a turn and start another. On steeps they may have an unsettling tendency to keep turning uphill and spin you around. Many off-piste, mogul, and "steep" skiers prefer modern shapes with a little less sidecut because of these disadvantages in gnarlier terrain.

But that's all theory—a sidecut number is only an index of how much sidecut is used in developing a ski's shape. It doesn't independently determine how the ski will perform, how quick it is, how it flexes, how easy-turning or stable it is, or how it holds. If the mix of these elements is blended properly, you can enjoy the benefits of more shape without sacrificing stability and off-piste performance.

So how do you tell what's too much? It depends on what you want to do. Very generally, for all-mountain—**freeride**—skiing, skis that are wider underfoot (say, at least 70 millimeters) can enjoy the benefits of more sidecut and still be very versatile. In modern lingo that's at least **mid-fat** dimensions, ranging into what many manufacturers refer to as **fat** skis. A ski that is

1
A sidecut ski

narrower underfoot, with more sidecut, usually means a more specialized **carving** ski.

My personal preference is this wider platform—at least 70 millimeters underfoot—with shape.

Camber and flex. Camber and **flex** combine to form the shape of a ski's flex (see illus. 2). Since we're talking about downhill performance, for the best turns, **alpine camber** is what we are looking for. When dry-land flexed, alpine-cambered skis should form a smooth arc, with no bumps, wiggles, or wax pockets. When skied, alpine camber flexes to distribute weight more evenly over the entire running surface of the ski. You get a rebound effect from turn to turn.

Nordic double camber is too stiff for making turns. The best example of nordic camber is the stiff, arched midsection of a classic-style cross-country racing ski. This stiff second camber creates a wax pocket that is pushed down onto the snow for purchase with the skier's kick. As the skier kicks with one ski he shifts his weight to the other ski—the gliding ski. The gliding ski slides on its slippery, glide-waxed tips and tails, its stiff wax pocket up off of the snow.

Backcountry touring skis, a category of skis used by many tourers who apply the techniques in this book, should *not* have this double camber. It's too stiff underfoot for round turning. What's wanted for this type of ski is a "camber and a half"—a bit of a wax pocket, but not a true second camber. That extra half helps the skis glide on the tips and tails without dragging the kick wax applied in that extra half-camber pocket. (Camber and a half still hinders a ski's turning—for the best turns alpine camber is the first choice.)

Stiffness of flex. Traditional thinking says that softer-flexing skis arc (flex into a curve to scribe a turn) more easily in softer snow. Stiffer skis are thought to be more stable and will edge better on hard snow but are slow to turn in powder. These rules of thumb have changed with new constructions that increase **torsional rigidity**—the ski's resistance to twisting along its long axis—and new designs with more shape (sidecut). These two characteristics combine to increase edge pressure and edge hold without the need to increase a ski's overall stiffness.

Today's best-performing all-around skis are torsionally rigid, with a medium-to-soft overall flex. There are exceptions: racers, skiers who frequent prepared piste, and those who live in climates with very hard snow conditions may choose a stiffer board.

I prefer medium-flexing skis—not too soft or stiff—with good torsional rigidity.

2
Camber

Ski Lengths

A ski doesn't know how *tall* you are, it knows how *heavy* you are. Forget those traditional lengths, as sidecut has so much effect on a ski's performance that it negates those once-standard measurements. Find out what length a men's "medium" is in the model that you're researching. A medium is the standard, most-used length for medium-sized men. In most of the newer shaped telemark skis, for example, that's around a 180 to 185, plus or minus a few centimeters. If you fall within that men's medium body type, that's your length. If you're large, go one length longer; small, one length shorter. A women's large corresponds to the men's small, so women go one length shorter for a women's large, two lengths for a medium, and so on.

If you are particularly heavy or light for your body size, you may go up or down a ski length—again, skis respond to weight, not height.

Extra-large men and smaller women may find fewer choices of ski models offered in an appropriate length. Ski molds are very expensive, and manufacturers don't normally build every ski model up to a 198 or 200 or down to a 165 or 170. If you fall into one of those categories, choose a model that's manufactured in your appropriate length. Or, often an extra-large skier can ski a stiffer ski in a shorter length, or an extra-small skier can use a softer ski in a longer length, to accommodate their sizes.

Types of Skis

Tele skis, randonnée skis, and alpine skis: what's the difference? Before stiff plastic boots and new ski shapes, there was a *big* difference. Alpine skis were long and heavy, tele skis were longer and skinny, and randonnée skis were short and fat. Today they all look the same: short, fat, and shaped. The real differences today are in what kind of skiing style and snow they are designed for. High-performance alpine skis tend to be of heavier, burlier construction for the added leverage of a fixed heel, a very stiff boot, and aggressive skiing. Tele and randonnée skis tend to be a bit lighter to accommodate a softer plastic boot in a less rigid binding system, and for easier touring and tighter-radius turns. The lines between these categories have blurred with modern technologies, as some of the most versatile skis can go either way. Aggressive tele skiers may mount up a more maneuverable alpine ski, off-piste alpine skiers may mount up a fat tele/randonnée crud-buster.

Overwhelmed? That is exactly why demo-ing before buying has become the norm in our industry. First, talk to your friends, those who like the kind of skiing that you like, and see what skis they prefer. Consult the magazine reviews to help narrow down your choices. Find a good shop with knowledgeable salespeople and ask them to show you a few skis. Getting them on snow is the real acid test, but using the journals and retail expertise, you can get an idea of the range of widths, shapes, and flexes that are available, and what skis you should test. Once you've narrowed it down, *try before you buy*.

POLES

The new composite-shaft poles are great. My favorite backcountry ones are adjustable, make an avalanche probe, have super-comfortable grips, and have interchangeable baskets for different snow climates. Even with all of their features, with a composite lower shaft they swing like a racing pole. They are expensive; if you don't want to spend that kind of money, or are worried about the durability of such skinny tubes, there are quality aluminum and, for the most durable, steel ones on the market with adjustability and the probe feature.

Note: For more severe terrain especially, I find little need to adjust my pole length because they aren't being used for propulsion. Adjustability is a plus, but first I look for the probe feature, the comfort of the grip, swing weight, and durability.

BOOTS

Most of today's boots have the traditional 75-millimeter toes, but that's their only resemblance to my long-retired lace-up leather touring boots. Today's most popular boots are plastic, with easy-to-use buckles and cozy removable inner boots, and most have a walk mechanism with different positions for walking freedom and downhill support. These new, high-tech plastic boots are warm, dry, comfortable, and durable.

Spend as much as you can afford on boots. If you have to compromise, do so somewhere else—sore feet mean no fun. Boots are the critical link between feet and skis.

Telemark boots should be as laterally stiff as possible for edge control with an easy, comfortable, natural fore-to-aft sole flex for telemark turning. Different manufacturers use different plastic injection technologies to achieve these characteristics. One of the strongest new technologies is the use of multiple injections. This process incorporates different stiffnesses of plastic into the same shell. These multiple injections allow the manufacturer to dial stiffness or softness into specific parts of the shell to increase torsional (lateral) rigidity while maintaining an easy forward flex.

Plastic boots come in different weights, heights, and flexes for different kinds of skiing. Each performs best when paired with a certain kind of ski. Most manufacturers make women's-specific versions of these boot models. Check out the illustrations.

3
Modern plastic boot designed for touring and backcountry telemarking

Illustration 3 shows a modern plastic boot designed for touring and backcountry telemarking. It has a lower, single-buckle cuff and a simple walk/forward lean locking mechanism. If you're not used to—or don't want—a high cuff, this boot is a good telemark choice. Many skiers with higher, stiffer boots for the resort have a pair of these lower models for touring. Although lower and softer, this style of boot still has more lasting torsional control than a leather boot. It's best to pair this style of boot with a lighter, easier-turning ski.

Illustration 4 is a higher, all-purpose model for all-round backcountry and resort skiing. They are plenty high for performance skiing with a one-buckle and Velcro® power strap cuff, and walk/locking mechanism. Women often prefer this height for calf comfort since many women's calf muscles reach lower down the leg. These boots are compatible with all but the biggest, heaviest skis.

4
All-purpose plastic boot for all-round backcountry and resort skiing

In illustration 5 you'll see the highest, stiffest, baddest kind of plastic boot for aggressive downhill-oriented skiing. They have two-buckle cuffs with a power strap, and use stiffer plastics throughout. They, too, have a walk mode, with a mechanism that locks with two choices of forward lean. These boots are compatible with wider, bigger, heavier boards for the most aggressive skiers.

Whatever model suits your skiing preference, its cuff should fit closely to your leg so that it can respond quickly to your movements. The forefoot should be snug enough to hold your foot securely, but not so narrow as to inhibit your foot's flex. You should be able to make teles by the dozen without smashing your toes against their ends, or suffering "toe pinch": flexing down of the boots against the tops of your toes. If you get toe pinch in a certain boot, try another size, model, or brand. And be sure that you have enough toe room to flex forward with little or no lift in the heel.

5
Plastic boot designed for aggressive, downhill-oriented skiing

Supportive footbeds are a must; especially important as skis get wider and boots get stiffer. Some boots come with an acceptable footbed as standard equipment. There are also off-the-shelf after-market models that function well. But the best footbeds are molded to your feet, designed specifically for skiers. For free-heel skiing you'll want a full-foot model rather than rear-foot only, since during the telemark turn you're putting a great deal of weight on the front part of your back foot. If you choose custom footbeds be sure that the forefoot area is built from a flexible material that can flex a zillion times without cracking.

For those seeking complete customization, there are several after-market inner boots that can be heated and molded to the exact shape of the foot. These custom liners are a bit less durable than conventional liners, and some models are less stiff, but they are extremely light, warm, and comfortable.

BINDINGS

Bindings, the only archaic part of the modern free-heel skier's kit, are changing rapidly. There are three general kinds of binding in use: three-pin bindings, cable bindings, and new step-in releasables like the ground-breaking Fritschi Skyhoy. Except for the Fritschi-type bindings, most late-model telemark bindings still incorporate a hundred-year-old concept.

Three-pin bindings, eclipsed by modern cable bindings, were once the standard (illus. 6). Although an ancient design, they offer a simple, no-nonsense attachment of boot to ski. The marriage of those little holes and the binding's three pins, however, is what takes all the stress of kicks, glides, turns, and head plants—and this marriage wasn't designed to endure the leverage generated by today's stiff boots. So I don't recommend three-pin bindings with stiff boots. However, if you do use three-pin bindings, I recommend those designed with supplemental cables for better boot support and longevity. And should you insist on using a "naked" pin binding with no cables, be sure that your boots have a secure, molded-in metal plate that reinforces the pinholes. Check the pinholes regularly for erosion. And carry an extra binding—three-pin bindings are notorious for breaking under the stresses of modern plastic boots.

Cable bindings are the most commonly used design for resort skiing and remote tours (illus. 7). They eliminate the dependence on three pins, plates, and pinholes. The cable adds more torsional rigidity to the boot for downhill control. Cable bindings are available that operate under a couple of different principles, with springs that *extend* when flexing the boot, or springs that *compress*—as in illustration 7—when flexing the boot. Especially with today's stiffer plastic boots, there are strong arguments for cable bindings with springs that compress with forward boot flex.

Before leaving on your trip, check to see that your cables are the right size for your boots and be sure that the cables are securely strapped together with the skis for transport. On tours, carry the appropriate adjustment wrench and a spare cable in your repair kit.

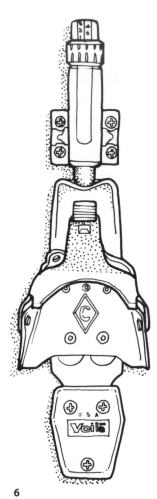

6

Three-pin binding with a retrofit release mechanism

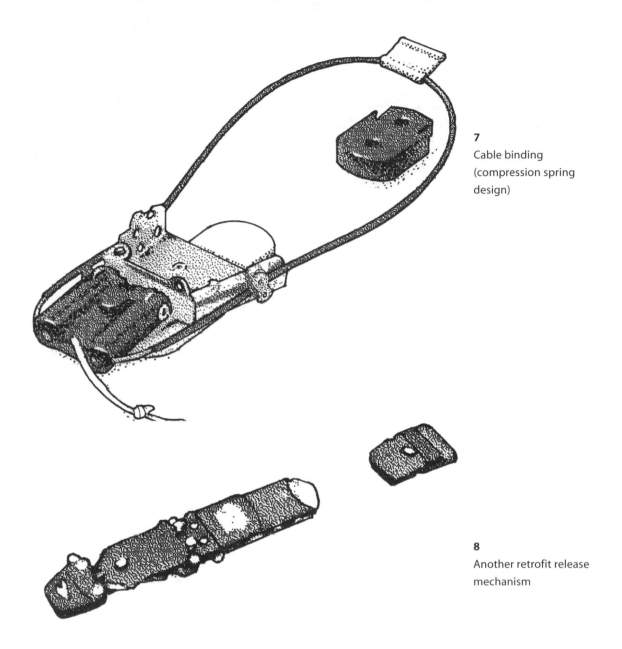

7
Cable binding
(compression spring
design)

8
Another retrofit release
mechanism

One way to improve the three-pin or cable bindings is by adding a retrofit release mechanism (illustrations 6 and 8). The release is designed to reduce injuries from tips hooked on gates during races or willows off the piste. The release system definitely adds more paraphernalia and weight to your system, but if safety is a priority over simplicity the releasable binding is an excellent choice.

Raising the binding and boot off of the ski with a riser plate is now the norm, especially with the advent of shaped skis. With a laterally stiff boot, these riser plates give you more leverage to hold the ski up on its edge to make use of all of that sidecut. And you need that leverage with wider skis. Risers raise the wings of the binding so that they (or the side of your boot) are less likely to catch and "wing out," a nasty phenomenon similar to catching a pedal on your bicycle in a tight corner. Many bindings come standard with riser plates, and there are numerous after-market riser plates available. As always, there are extremes, but the height norm for all-round skiing seems to be about a 20–25 millimeter riser. Racers ski on risers as high as 40 millimeters, but that gets you pretty far away from what's going on. The most secure mounting system is a riser that first mounts to the ski, and then the binding mounts to the riser. This double-mount system is imperative with stiff boots.

And last, the future: **step-in releasable bindings.** Fritschi, well-known for some of the best randonnée bindings available, has developed the first of its kind for aggressive free-heel skiing (see illus. 9). All of the important points

9

Step-in releasable
binding

listed above, and more, are combined into one unit: leverage, safety, ease of use, releasability, and the riser. One of its disadvantages is weight—certainly these bindings are much heavier than a naked cable binding. (One could argue that once you combine the features of a conventional binding, riser, and add-on release mechanism, the weight is comparable.) Another disadvantage is flex. By definition, the step-in design that uses a toe and heel requires a plate to connect the two, and this can inhibit or change your boot's flex. And a final disadvantage is price, although like the weight argument, if you combine all the features of a Skyhoy using the more conventional system (bindings, risers, retrofit release) you have probably spent a comparable amount of money.

I mount all of my skis with heel plates that include heel lifters. Heel lifters are indispensable for steep climbing with skins, significantly reducing lower leg and ankle fatigue. The lifter usually consists of a heavy wire bail that can be flipped up to elevate your heel when ascending steep slopes. Lifters allow you to distribute your weight over your whole foot so that climbing steep slopes is like climbing stairs. Most of the best riser plates include a heel plate with a lifter option (see illus. 10).

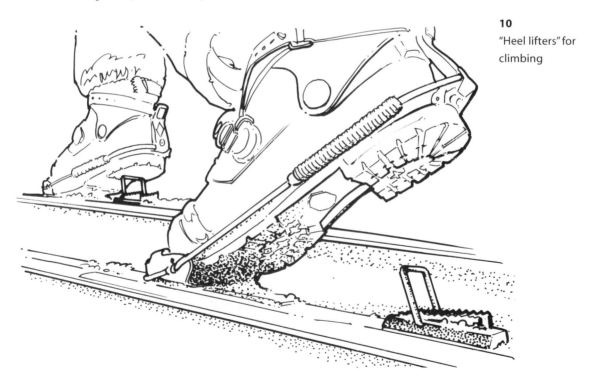

10
"Heel lifters" for climbing

MOUNTING TELE BINDINGS

Where do you mount tele bindings? I use the chord length of the ski—the old balance point theory is irrelevant when mounting a metal-edged, sidecut ski. Measure the length of the ski in a straight line across its topsheet, from the tip to the tail (see illus. 11). Divide this number in half, measure that distance from the tail, and mark it on the top of the ski. That mark is the chord center of the ski. I have average-sized boots, and test a lot of skis, so I mount all of my bindings so that the boot's pinholes are on that chord center mark. "Pins on chord center" is what I think of as the neutral mounting point, what is best-suited for my testing needs. Many knowledgeable skiers mount their bindings ahead 1 centimeter to (theoretically) make the skis a bit easier to initiate a turn, with a little more tail to finish the turn. This system works fine, although I must admit that it's difficult to tell the difference.

Note: Even though most of us use cables, the boot-pinhole position is a reference point shown on most binding mounting jigs.

One important element is boot size. The average size of a man's boot is 31 centimeters from the toe (pinholes) to the heel. If your boots are much shorter or longer than that, and you tend toward the technical, it's worth adjusting your mounting position for your boot length to get your body mass in the correct place on the ski. To do this, mark chord center as described above. Measure your boot sole length from pinholes to heel. If that number is different from 31 centimeters, calculate the difference. If it's longer than 31 centimeters, for every centimeter *longer*, mark the ski *one half centimeter (5 millimeters) ahead* of your chord center mark, and mount the binding with the boot pinholes there. If your boot is shorter than 31 centimeters, for every centimeter *shorter*, mark the ski *one half centimeter (5 millimeters) behind* your chord center mark, and mount the binding with the boot pinholes there. What that half-centimeter does is split the difference from the average— 31 centimeters—to keep your body over the center of the ski, regardless of your boot size.

SKINS

Several years ago a group of us flew in to a remote Canadian hut to backcountry ski. One of my buddies, a randonnée skier, chose a pair of what were then new-wave fat skis that were more than 100 millimeters wide at their tips. (It wasn't so long ago that 100 millimeters was way fat!) The first day he took them out was a big tour, with over 2000 meters of climbing (and descending). We were all tired at the end of that day, but he was doubly

11
Chord length

hammered, having constantly struggled all day to maintain uphill traction. He'd slip even in a well-packed, dry-snow, no-traverse skin track, and he virtually skated when the track traversed. His skins, plenty wide for his traditional randonnée skis, exposed too much base underfoot when mounted on these fat boys, and slipped desperately.

Skins are for traction. I don't try to save weight or increase glide with a narrower skin width. To get the best 4x4 performance, choose ones that are wide enough to cover the skis edge-to-edge at the narrowest point. You need only the metal edge exposed.

If you use shaped skis in the backcountry, even with this "narrowest point/edge-to-edge" rule of thumb you'll have a lot of base exposed. I recommend getting shaped skis their own pair of super-wide skins. Several manufacturers make big ones, and many have a simple cutting kit that allows you to custom-cut sidecut into the skin to cover as much of the skis' base as is practical while keeping the edge visible. You want the skin edge-to-edge for about the middle two-thirds of the ski, so you can measure the ski about 25–30 centimeters back from the tip, and buy that skin width. Then follow the trimming instructions to cut the ski's sidecut into the skin.

The most popular skins are made from a synthetic and/or mohair plush pile that is designed to perform like natural sealskin—the original skin material. With hairs that point back, the skin can slide forward; but when pushed back, the hairs are pushed against their grain to dig into the snow surface. Mohair skins are said to glide better in cold weather. Synthetic skins are generally more durable. Both types of plush perform very well.

Most of today's skins use a renewable adhesive that sticks to a clean ski base with very little additional hardware. Unlike the old strap-on skins, they do not accumulate snow underneath and slip sideways, and the ski edges are exposed for side-stepping and hard-snow traverses. Many adhesive skins have tip loops and tail hooks, with elastic at one end or the other. If the skins are properly glued and carefully applied to the ski, this hardware isn't necessary, but it does help keep the skins from sliding off of the tail. With an elastic/tail-hook system, it's important not to adjust the skin length too short; you'll put too much tension on the skin and actually work against the adhesive.

To get the best performance from your skins, take care of them. Scrape excess wax off of your skis. Wipe the ski base clean of dirt and moisture before putting on the skins. When carrying skins, fold them back on themselves, adhesive-against-adhesive, so that your stick-um is not contaminated (see illus. 12). Be careful not to drop your skins in the pine needles.

The newest skin adhesives are extraordinarily durable, remaining

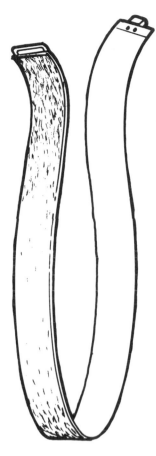

12
Folding skins

effective for many, many applications. How many depends on temperature and how clean you keep them. I used to reglue my skins before any big trip, but with the new stuff it seems like I rarely need to reglue more than once a season.

Regluing skins can be like applying klister on a squirmy, moving target. It's a bit easier if you duct-tape them by the tip and tail attachments, glue side up, to an easily cleaned workbench or tabletop. Be sure to pull them tight. Old glue comes off easily with a hot knife, peeling right off the backing. Or you can warm it with a hair dryer and carefully remove it with a scraper. Either way, be careful not to get the skin material too hot, or cut the material with sharp edges.

New glue should be warm when applied. Deposit a bead sparingly in the center of the skin and spread it with a putty knife. If this all sounds like a mess, many shops—and some skin distributors—are set up to reglue your skins for a nominal fee. And some manufacturers have developed an iron-on regluing system that is clean and easy.

BACKPACKS

I've often found myself trying to cram my boots into a too-small pack so that I could make a long approach in my tennies. So my favorite pack is big enough to carry my boots. When it's not full, it sucks down nice and small, compact and close to my back with compression straps compressed. I find this size of pack, about 40–50 liters, more versatile than most for ski mountaineering because there is plenty of room for bulky down jackets in winter, boots in spring, and full mountaineering gear for glacier travel on long hut-to-hut tours.

Compression straps are critical, both to compress the pack and stabilize the load, and as attachment points to carry skis. I prefer a pack with a bag sewn in a lighter-weight fabric and one that doesn't have too many extra features on the outside or too heavy a suspension. It's easy to agonize over every ounce of a pack's contents and then cancel out the effort with a 6-pound receptacle. Ice ax and ski attachments are about all that you need.

The one extra feature that I have found useful for a backcountry skiing pack is a zipper that allows access to the lower part of the pack bag. It's especially useful when skis are strapped on the pack, hindering access into the bag. On ski mountaineering trips it's good to carry the heavy, less frequently used gear like ropes and crampons in the bottom, keeping the pack's center of gravity low. A zipper allows fast access to these heavier pieces, which is usually what you want when you need this kind of hardware. When you need your crampons or rope, you need them *now*.

WHAT TO TAKE TO THE BACKCOUNTRY

A light pack means more fun when backcountry skiing. For that reason, I'm usually as worried about what I can leave behind as what to take when planning a ski trip. So through the years, besides my poles (see Important Gear I've Forgotten, p. 41), I've forgotten a few important items. These days I always try to run through a few things in my mind before heading out.

- **Skis and poles** (the big stuff!)
- *Harscheisen.* German for ski crampons, *harscheisen* are indispensable on firm glacier tours and in crusty high-alpine conditions. They are a bit harder to find for tele skis. In Europe there are separate *harscheisen* (called *couteau* in French, *cortelli* in Italian) available that will work on tele boards, mounting separately from the AT binding (Petzl is one). Rainey Designs offers a *harscheisen* option with their telemark binding.
- **Skins**
- **Backpack**
- **Smaller essentials.** There are key essentials—at least 10 of them—that should not be left behind. Here are several that I carry in my personal kit:

    Gaiters. You need some sort of gaiter to keep the snow out of your boots. For simplicity, I prefer shell pants or stretch-type mountaineering pants with a built-in gaiter or sturdy elasticized cuff that seals boot tops. Whether part of your pants or a separate accessory, gaiters should form a secure seal around your boots' uppers.

    Thermos. I love having something hot to drink when it's cold, and usually carry a small, lightweight thermos for my backcountry trips. I like the bullet-shaped metal kind. They aren't that heavy, and if you look hard you can even find titanium ones that weigh little more than a plastic water bottle. One note of caution—these suckers are slippery, and disappear down a firm snow (or tundra) slope as fast as a loose ski. Tape a handle on it, or just be careful with it.

    Eyewear. I'm into goggles for skiing downhill. For the backcountry, I use a pair with bigger frames for minimal fog, and flexible lenses that are less likely to break. I use a Tupperware®-type box for them from the grocery store (a couple of bucks) that gives them more rigid protection.

    I find the new-style sunglasses with interchangeable lenses absolutely invaluable. In flat light conditions—often the case when the skiing's the best—you can easily change from dark to yellow or rose lenses that significantly improve your depth perception. They are less likely to fog than goggles when you're working hard, and you'll find them great for mountain biking in the summer when you're going from sun to shade.

© Paul Parker

Important Gear
that I've Forgotten

~

Shivering in the cold, raw wind on the top of the Julier Pass, my partner and I hurriedly put on our skins and clicked into our skis. Simultaneously, we turned to reach for our poles. They were nowhere to be seen.

The driver had just driven away, having left us at the trailhead for the Swiss Albula tour. At the hotel, he'd offered to load our skis while we took off our ice axes to load our packs in his taxi. He must not have known that skis and poles make a set, all leaning together against the hotel building. We couldn't believe it, at the start of a tour without our poles, knowing that it would be a couple of hours and two more $50 cab rides to go down and back to get them.

Until our pole dilemma, we were feeling pretty good about ourselves, having gotten out of incredibly expensive St. Moritz in less than a day. We'd arrived the afternoon before from the States, and in only a couple of hours that morning we'd packed, bought some odds and ends, and reserved our blankets in the Jenatsch Hutte. Since the bus wasn't running, we'd needed a taxi to the top of the pass. Now, standing at the trailhead as I swore profusely, we felt stranded and jet-lagged.

Two friendly-looking German women were nearby, eyeing us and our frustration as they prepared to start the same tour. Wanting to help, one of them came over and offered me a ride to a nearby roadside rifugio. She needed to call the hut and make reservations, and suggested that I call the hotel and see if the poles were there.

"Oh Dio!" the young girl at our hotel exclaimed; they were there. Could she put them behind the desk for me?

As I pondered what I was going to do, this generous woman suggested that I borrow her car and drive the half hour each way to St. Moritz for the poles. I could give her the keys in the hut that night. Can you imagine making such an offer to a perfect stranger? She didn't even know if I had a driver's license! Incredulous, I was delighted that she'd offered.

It worked. I got the poles, we were on our way, and made the hut by dark.

You may not find such a generous, trusting soul. Don't forget your poles.

They've changed my life—no longer do I feel like Ray Charles when skiing's the best!

Shovels and avalanche beacons are critical. Beacons should have compatible frequencies; the newer single-frequency 457 Hz (now the international standard) units are the most powerful. The new digital units have very advanced directional locating systems and are, in general, easier to use. *Be sure that your groups' beacons work together, and know how to use them. Check their batteries before each trip. Carry extra batteries for extended trips.*

Note: I recommend that *every* backcountry rider take an in-depth avalanche course. Educate yourself, and be conservative.

Routefinding aids. No one is immune to getting lost. Routefinding is a key element on all backcountry trips. One would think, for example, that European hut trips have few routefinding challenges. On spring tours like Chamonix–Zermatt there is a highway between huts. Don't be too confident; snow falls, blows in the tracks, and then the fog sets in. Some of my most challenging routefinding has been on well-traveled alpine tours, finding a hut at the terminus of a foggy glacier with a big drop at the end and ice cliffs on both sides.

Unless I'm in my backyard, I carry a map, compass, and altimeter at all times. Be sure to calibrate the altimeter at a known point each day or it's useless. Know how to use it, and your compass, and be able to read a map well. *Refer to your map often.* Keep it in a handy place where it's no hassle to get at it frequently. Those who own a Global Positioning System (GPS) should be familiar with its use, but don't depend solely on the satellites. Carry a backup compass, and don't forget your altimeter— in heavy fog there is no substitute.

Repair kit. Put together a repair kit with spare binding parts, wire, duct tape, and a screwdriver that fits all of your binding screws (and any other important gear, like crampons). For quick, simple repairs you can wrap a bit of duct tape around the upper portion of your ski poles, close to the grip so that you don't notice its weight. On extended trips take sewing paraphernalia and skin glue. I try to keep my repair kit small and minimal, and leave it in my pack so that I don't forget it.

Note: I've seen several little pocket screwdriver kits in snowboard shops that have every kind of bit you'd need. One of these may fit the bill for your repair kit.

First-aid kit. A small first-aid kit is another essential to store in your pack. An elastic bandage, first-aid tape (also good for taping skins that pop off), plastic strip bandages, antibiotic ointment, and, most importantly, a blister kit are in my "minimal" kit. This is another item that I keep small and light, and it lives in the pack.

Matches and a butane lighter.

Something warm. I dress in layers from the inside, the first few layers being the most crucial for staying dry and comfortable. I have a favorite outfit that I work from, adding and subtracting according to season. My basic outfit includes moisture-managing underwear, a combination windshirt-underwear top, appropriate insulating layers, and protective shell layers. The shells are lightweight—unless you're ice or rock climbing you don't need much abrasion resistance. In addition, in my pack there's always an extra-warm insulating jacket for breaks, summits of peak climbs, and unplanned events. There are all sorts of down and synthetic pieces on the market that fit this need. My only advice is to choose something that will keep you warm when fairly inactive, yet that's lightweight enough so that you will never mind taking it along. I have a superlight down sweater that I take in spring, and a puffier down parka for winter trips. A hood attached to both of these pieces makes them far warmer with little additional weight and bulk.

- **Make a list.** Finally, once you've put your favorite kit together, make a list. You can edit it over time should you wish you'd had something, or find you've never used a piece of gear. You'll find it much easier and quicker to pack for that pre-dawn alpine start. And you're less likely to forget something important, like your poles.

Photo on following pages
© Ace Kvale

FOUNDATION
SKILLS

Wedge Turns

Most metal-edged skis are meant to turn. Their designs vary widely and determine how eager a ski is to turn. In general, more sidecut means more eager. Why? The waist of a sidecut ski is narrower than the tip and tail, so when it is put on its edge and weighted, it will flex into an arc. Form that arc while moving and your ski will describe a turn (see illus. 13).

The size of the turn scribed by a weighted, sidecut ski, with no other help from the skier, doesn't always fit the terrain. To avoid slamming into things, you'll have to learn how to tighten and vary your turns. Below I describe skills that add or reduce pressure on the skis, making them easier to turn. You'll learn to turn them by "steering" the skis actively with feet that are alive and moving, and you'll use the skis' edges.

Wedge turns are some of the most important turns you will learn. You'll always fall back on them, even after you've mastered telemark and parallel turns. You'll use them daily to get on lifts, to avoid other skiers, or to pick your way down a corniced ridge. Ski patrollers use wedge turns to control their sleds and to get injured skiers safely down the hill. Learn them well.

Wedge turns aren't snowplow turns. They evolved from the snowplow, look similar, and many might think that they are the same. But the snowplow is an older "braking" turn—an effective one—with tips very close together and tails far apart. Wedge turns are more fluid, with more gliding, more maneuverability, and a less defensive stance. Your feet aren't static; they are moving all of the time: alive.

Photo on preceding page
© Scott Cramer

BODY POSITION

You'll need to maintain an effective athletic stance throughout all of these techniques—a stable, relaxed, in-balance position that frees your body to act and react quickly and easily. Try it: relax your back muscles and "cup" your upper body, pulling your navel in toward your backbone. Feel your weight centered squarely on both feet.

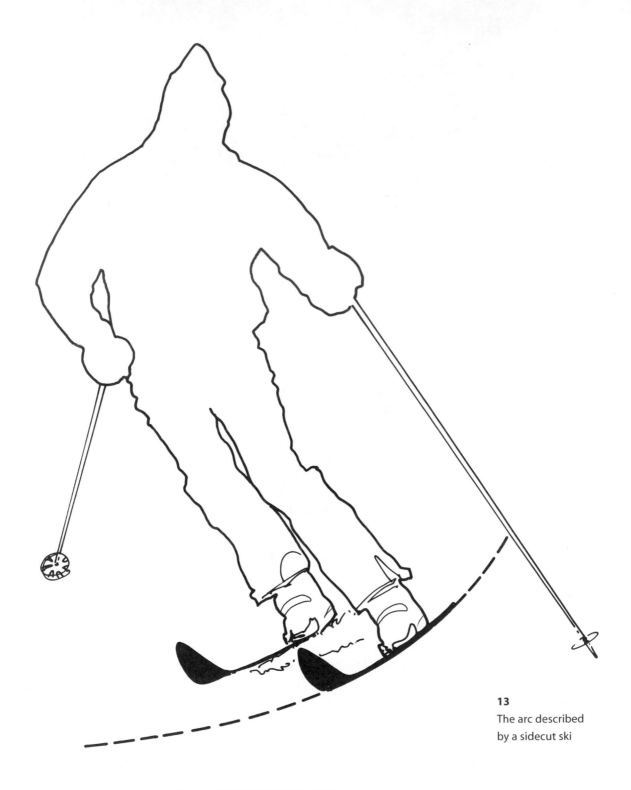

13
The arc described
by a sidecut ski

The stability test: assume the stance I've described. Rock back and forth from your toes to your heels. Now try it the wrong way: arch your back, tense it, and rock back and forth. Which way feels more balanced? Which way would you catch a basketball? There's no substitute for a round, relaxed back.

I always use this athletic stance. I think especially hard about it whenever the skiing is difficult. It keeps my back from hurting. It's a familiar focus to rely on, one that always works. When I lose my balance to the rear, this stance helps me get out of a desperate position—the "back seat." It "collects" my body into a stable, strong position.

GETTING STARTED

Let's get on snow. Put your skis on in a flat spot where you can practice a few exercises. First, lift one foot, then the other. Get the feel of having skis on your feet. Raise your toes, then point them down. Standing on one foot, point your ski tip to the right, then to the left. Change feet and repeat.

Now, from a solid stance on both feet, hop your ski tails into a wedge. Your toes should be pointed inward, your hips, shoulders, and head centered between the skis. Your ski tips should be several inches apart. This is a wedge position.

THE STRAIGHT RUN

Here's a term that might be new to you: **fall line.** The fall line is the direction a ball would roll when tossed down a slope. It's gravity's choice, the most direct downhill-sloping path. Some call it the "fun line." Find a very gentle slope, ski-packed or groomed, with a good runout. Pick an obstacle-free fall line on your slope. Start with the correct body position, your athletic stance: stomach in, back round and relaxed, ankles flexed with knees forward. Keep your eyes on the road ahead—not on your ski tips.

Point your skis down the hill and ready . . . Go! Push off with your poles for momentum. Skis should be parallel at about hip width (see top figure in illus. 14). Let your skis run straight to the bottom. Keep your ankles and knees flexed and relaxed. Keep your weight centered on your feet, both side-to-side and fore-to-aft.

If that was too easy, we'll make it more interesting. Take another straight run, but this time, shuffle your feet back and forth without lifting your heels. Try standing on one foot, then another. Hop up and down. Go back to a shuffle. You want to feel as though your feet are mobile, flexible, loose, not stuck in a static position. That's what I mean by feet that are alive.

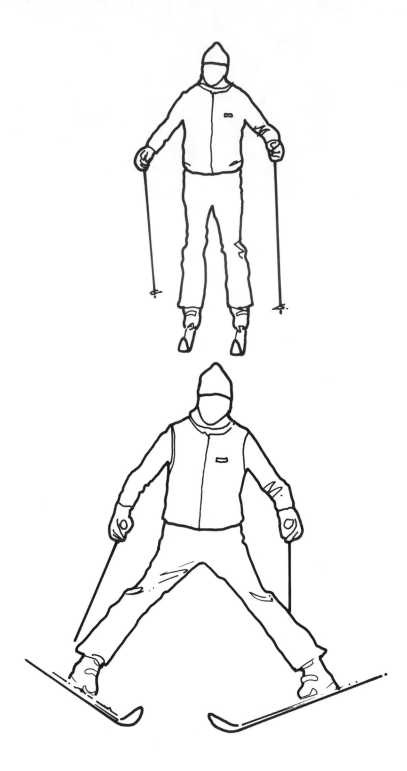

14
Straight run to
a wedge

THE WEDGE

Try it again, but this time, gently push your heels out, keeping your toes pointed inward. Don't worry about using your edges; stay light on them. It should feel as though you are *brushing* the skis out into a wedge, not grinding them. Let your skis glide as you brush them out, pushing your heels away from you. Are they in a wedge? Now widen your wedge by pushing on your heels; see if you can brake to a stop (see illus. 14).

Experiment with the width of your wedge. See what happens when you brush your ski tails farther apart, then let them glide closer together.

It's important when using a wedge not to lock your knees together. Keep them apart, as though you were riding a horse or holding a soccer ball or even a basketball between them. Do the same with your ski tips: keep them apart, almost a soccer ball's width. If your tips want to cross, begin your wedge with your feet farther apart, at hip width.

To slow down, push out on your heels and widen the wedge. This is the "braking" wedge: as your feet widen, your skis tip over more onto their edges. This "edging" puts on the brakes.

Use this wedge width to vary the braking action—wider for more braking, narrower for less. Just take care to avoid locked knees when you put on the brakes.

Flex your ankles, pressing on the inside edges. Don't roll your ankles inward: just flex them, pressing on those edges. Now vary the wedge: go back and forth from a narrow wedge with more glide to a wide wedge with more edge and braking action. Feel your speed change as increased edging slows you down, decreased edging speeds you up. Imagine that a tree just appeared in front of you, and make an emergency stop.

Note: if you are having trouble slowing yourself to a stop, tighten your boots. Think of pressure building under the big-toe sides of both feet.

DOING A WEDGE TURN

Let's try a turn. Let your skis run to get some momentum and then sink into a wedge—this time a narrow one to keep your speed. Next, exaggerate the wedging movement with one foot; press harder on one foot as you wedge it. Think of squashing a bug under the ball of your foot. You will turn in the direction that your squashing foot is pointing. That means that squashing with your right foot turns you left. Squashing with the left foot turns you right (see illus. 15).

From now on, in all of your turns, I'll refer to this squashing foot—the turning foot (and ski)—as the *outside foot* (and ski). It's called that because it is on the outside of your turn's arc. You will also hear this foot called the *downhill foot*—it is on the downhill side of the turn. In the illustration, the skier's squashing foot is highlighted.

To link your turns, gather some speed and alternate your squashing feet. Make shallow little arcs. Turn only with your feet, not with your upper body. Shift pressure from one foot to another. Be sure to keep your ankles and knees flexed and relaxed. Make some snaky S curves down the hill. Try controlling your speed with repeated turns. Get up some steam at the top; then try to slow down by turning in a narrow, gliding wedge. Even when you

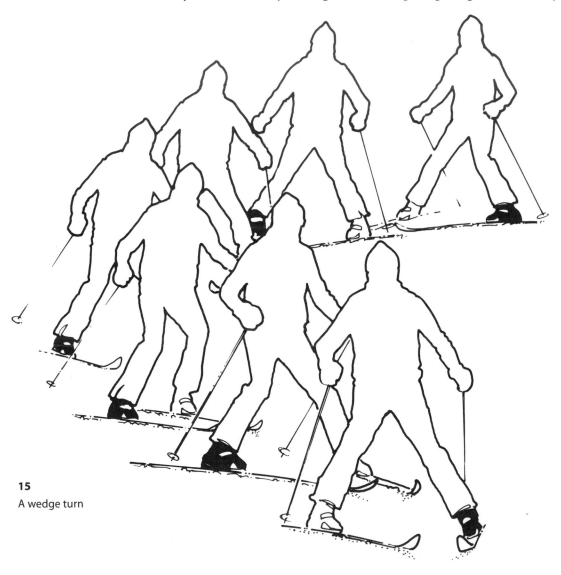

15
A wedge turn

use less edging, turning out of the fall line will slow you down (see illus. 16).

Now make another run and widen your wedge, controlling your speed with your edges. Feel how the edges control your speed?

Next try moving up and down. Rise up between turns and squash down on that foot to turn. Rise up and squash down, up, down.

Once you've got it, practice so that it sinks in. Vary your wedge width and turn size. Make a few wide turns, a few narrow ones, then wide ones again. With these skills you are using the braking wedge, the gliding wedge, and the wedge turn.

16
Linked wedge turns

Basic Telemark

Sondre Norheim, the father of the telemark, first used his telemark as a stable landing position after a long jump. Who knows? Maybe Norheim felt himself yanked forward landing an 80-meter jump and instinctively made a telemark as a survival measure to avoid a nasty face-plant. However it happened, Norheim's landing stance gave him fore-to-aft stability.

My first experience telemarking was in 1971, in the little town ski area north of Gunnison, Colorado. I don't remember much about it, just some confusion about which foot went forward when turning. I do remember my skis, a narrow pair of wooden Splitkeins.

My next memory is more vivid. It was a few days later, in Crested Butte. The day was perfect, warm and sunny on Snodgrass Mountain. There were five or six inches of light snow on a firm base.

I picked a nice-looking slope, waxed my skis, and packed a good climbing track up the hill. By then I had figured out which foot to put forward, but the first couple of times that I stuck out a lead ski not much happened— just huge arcs to a stop. Then it worked. I turned my front foot a little more with the turn and made my first telemark. What a feeling! I could only turn one way, though, so my next goal was to copy my movements in the other direction.

Why had I chosen to learn telemark? I had a dream of doing everything— uphill and downhill, backcountry and piste—on one kind of ski.

You don't have to be a jumper—or a dreamer—to appreciate the tele. It's a great choice in cruddy snow, very deep powder, or any conditions that yank your feet back while throwing your body forward. The telemark's genuflecting position has superior fore-to-aft stability. It braces the skier to help prevent uncomfortable forward falls.

It is easiest to learn telemarks, or any ski turn for that matter, through a logical learning progression. The following section is a skill progression to

Photo on preceding page
© Mark Shapiro

teach you a variety of necessary moves: the telemark position, the lead change, the shuffle or half-wedge turn, and the basic tele turn. If you take enough time with each skill, they will all work like building blocks toward your goal.

I'm going to give you some options for learning the basic telemark from a striding position or a half-wedge position. Try both and plug in to the one that works best for you. I've tried to be spare with the language. You will learn much better if you have a brief explanation of what to do, feel it and discover for yourself, and then study tips for improvement as you progress and develop your own questions.

THE TELEMARK STANCE

Your body position is fundamental. Start on a flat spot with the telemark stance, using your athletic body position: a round, relaxed back and a cupped stomach. Sink into a tele. Sink straight down, sliding one foot forward and one foot back. *Your weight should stay evenly distributed between both feet.* Experiment with a very tall stance and a very low stance, and find a comfortable spot in the middle. You should feel your weight resting on your whole front foot and on the ball of your rear foot (see illus. 17).

17
The telemark stance

LEARNING THE TELEMARK FROM A STRIDING POSITION

Learning the telemark from a striding position is a method that has withstood the test of time. It originated from a diagonal stride, the classic cross-country stride. But even if you have heard of this before, please pay attention to the one way that my explanation differs from this walking/skiing stride: *arms*. This is important: stride with your feet, not with your arms. Don't swing your arms as you do in a cross-country stride. Simply keep them relaxed and a bit in front of you (see illus. 18).

18
Striding into a telemark

In the flats, stride from one telemark position to another, taking exaggerated, bent-legged strides. Move as though you're trying to stay low and invisible in tall grass. It should be as much a sense of dropping down as it is of striding forward. You should be getting a good quad workout.

OK, now the hill. You'll need a good practice slope. The best practice terrain is a ski-area beginner's slope that is well packed and groomed. If you are lucky, the slope will have a slow-moving lift. If a lift is not available, find a gentle slope with a flat, obstacle-free runout. Pack the loose snow by side-stepping up and down the slope.

Pick a very gentle downhill that you can straight-run without fear. Point your skis straight down the slope, push off, and make those same striding moves straight down the hill. Terrain selection is important for this exercise; the goal here is a slow downhill on a slight incline that allows you to run straight with your skis flat.

Time out for a couple of new terms. First, **steering.** Steering is physically turning your ski—I call it "pointing" the ski with your foot. If you didn't already learn it in the section on wedge turns, the second term you need to know is **fall line.** It's the line a ball would take if you rolled it down a hill. When skiers say "step into the fall line," or "face down the fall line," they mean "step directly down the hill," or "face down the hill."

Now you're ready to try a telemark turn. At the same time that you stride into a new telemark position, steer (twist) your front foot into a turn. Remember that, just as in the wedge, the foot that you're pointing is the outside foot, and you're pointing it to the inside of the turn. Try turns one at a time, on each side. Turn your skis across the hill until you come to a stop. As you progress, think not only of your foot, but point your ski, foot, and knee into the turn (refer back to illus. 18).

As you gain confidence, on your easiest slope, start striding from turn to turn. Make your turns smaller, using the striding motion practiced above, steering each forward foot (and ski and knee) inside the turn. Once you get your balance, you'll find yourself striding from little tele to little tele, making S curves. Your front foot will feel more active as you stride, but don't forget your rear foot. Stride into each tele with fifty-fifty weight distribution.

LEARNING THE TELEMARK FROM A HALF-WEDGE

This is another option for learning the basics. My first exposure to the half-wedge approach was through my PSIA Nordic Demonstration Team coach. The coach, a longtime downhill instructor, showed me how this alpine-style idea was likely to avert the classic bad habits that plague the neophyte telemarker.

Begin with a straight run on your practice slope. Point one ski straight and wedge the other ski out (see illus. 19).

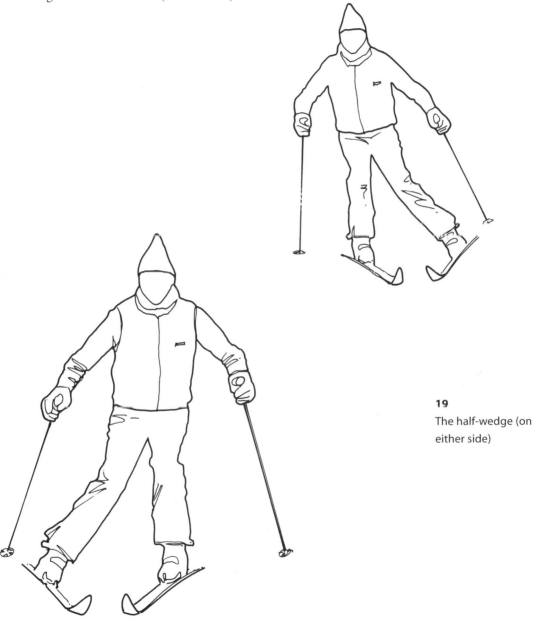

19
The half-wedge (on either side)

A note about weight: don't weight the wedged ski too much; you should feel its edge lightly brush against the snow. Your weight should remain focused on the straight-running ski. You'll find that although your weight is on your straight-running ski, the pressure that develops on the wedged ski initiates a direction change. To make turns, press harder against the wedged ski. Try these little turns on either side, keeping most of the weight on the straight-running ski but pressing against that wedged one.

OK, time out for more terms. From now on I'll refer to the straight-running ski as your **inside ski**, since it's the ski on the inside once you make a turn. The wedged ski I'll call the **outside ski**—it's the turning ski on the outside of the arc.

Make S curves, rhythmically linking shallow half-wedge turns (see illus. 20). Your weight will shift as your inside ski changes to your outside ski; as your weight moves to the new inside ski, the outside ski's edge brushes the snow and pulls you into a turn. You'll have the sensation that your legs are swinging back and forth under your body.

The transition from half-wedges to telemarks is the next step. Begin making half-wedge turns. As you wedge the outside ski, slide it forward and sink into the telemark stance. (Some skiers prefer to think of sliding the inside ski back rather than the outside ski forward. Try it and see which works for you.)

As you sink into that telemark stance, steer (point) the advanced front ski through a turn. Practice one turn at a time, beginning in a traverse and turning uphill to a stop. (What's a traverse? A **traverse** is gliding across the hill using your uphill edges to maintain a horizontal course.) Sink between your feet, with both skis equally weighted. Practice this "stop-turn" in both directions.

GARLANDS

Using either the striding-to-tele approach or the half-wedge-to-tele, once you become more comfortable turning to a stop in each direction you are ready to practice a garland. The exercise is named for the pattern your skis scribe in the snow. It's done by executing a series of stop-turns, progressively beginning each turn more in the fall line. It's a very useful way to develop confidence in your turns.

Start by picking a shallow, traversing line and turn uphill to a stop. As your confidence grows, step into the fall line a little more each time you begin a new stop-turn. Each turn starts with less traverse until finally there is no traverse at all. Once you are comfortable turning without a traverse, step directly down the hill, beginning the stop-turn in the fall line (see illus. 21).

20
Shallow half-wedge turns

21

A half-wedge into a
tele-garland

LINKING TURNS

On the easier part of your slope, try linking some stride- or wedge-teles down the hill. Sink into the telemark position at the same time you steer that front foot, knee, and ski. On a gentle slope you will feel as though you are walking "pigeon-toed" from one tele to the next. Steer your front foot more to make a tighter turn and slow down, steer less to speed up.

MOTION

With practice, you will find yourself thinking less of strides or half-wedges and more of a tele-to-tele movement. You'll pick up this sensation more quickly if you practice on very moderate slopes. As the slope steepens, you'll need to tele-turn your skis across the hill to check your speed. Then the transition to the next turn becomes more defined, a determined move into each successive telemark. To ease this transition and make each upcoming turn effective, you'll need to amplify what skiers simply call **motion** or **movement.** Remember my earlier reference to feet that are *alive?* This is the next step—motion that brings your *whole body* alive to smoothly get those skis around.

This movement is the key to linking your turns smoothly. Simplified, you could call it "up-and-down" movement. But it's not really that simple. It's dynamic movement—up, down, forward, and back; never static; never in a "position."

The purpose is to use your body's entire range of motion. Try it: stand tall at the beginning of your turn—much taller than in the classic telemark position you first practiced. Then sink through each tele turn as you make your arc, finishing the turn in that "classic" stance. Exaggerate tall and small. Stand up tall for the next turn and repeat the sinking motion through the arc.

As you sink, steer and edge your front ski. Each time you initiate a new turn, stand up again, sink, and steer. Your weight should be on the inside (uphill) edges of both skis. Feel the difference that the motion makes? Soon you'll be gracefully linking telemark turns one after another.

Basic Parallel Turns

Ilove parallel turns. Some of my buddies say that I'm cheating. There is no such thing as cheating. Anyway, if they could do them they'd probably cheat, too.

Parallel turns work. They are stable and efficient. They are remarkable on the steeps. Learn them to be an all-around skier.

One ski season years ago, I set a goal to improve my free-heel parallel turns. I skied as much as possible with alpine skiers, watching and mimicking them. I began to use parallel turns in more varied conditions. First I practiced parallels only on hard snow, where the skis were easy to steer. I made the most of the technique's stable side-to-side stance. As my turns became stronger I mixed them up, using them where least appropriate, trying to strengthen my parallel turns in powder and crud. Of course, I augured a lot, but I kept working at it. By the end of the season my parallels were coming around.

Why parallel? When terrain is steep, icy, or the space very tight for turning, parallel and other alpine techniques work great. The parallel's compact stance allows quick and efficient direction changes. Parallels are deceptively quick turns—and they are elegant.

Teles and parallels aren't all there is. To be a versatile, go-anywhere skier on all kinds of equipment you'll need to master a variety of maneuvers: wedges, wedge christies, stem christies, and parallels. Approached one by one, these moves form an ideal learning progression for developing the necessary foundation for strong, advanced parallel turns.

Photo on preceding page
© Scott Cramer

WEDGE AND STEM CHRISTIES

After wedge turns, **wedge christies** and **stem christies** are two of the skills that will build your foundation for strong parallel turns. Stem christies are often used at this stage for skiers who must learn on more difficult terrain and in ungroomed snow. The stem christy is initiated with one ski actively *stemmed* (wedged) out into a V—almost stepped into the V. The turn is finished with the skis *matched*, or parallel. The parallel skid that finishes the turn is called a **christy.**

Wedge christies move both skis together. In both turns, your skis move from wedge to parallel position. A culinary image you can keep in mind is "pizza (wedge or stem), fries (two parallel french fries), pizza, fries, pizza, fries." In working toward parallel, I'd recommend practicing both, starting first with wedge christies.

DOING A WEDGE CHRISTY

Make some short-radius wedge turns in the fall line. Be sure that your ski tips aren't too close together. Like your knees, your ski tips should have almost a soccer ball's width between them. A smaller-sized wedge—less of a V-shape—works best for these shorter turns.

Work on the shape of your wedge turn. You'll need a bit more speed. Think about making very *round* turns instead of shallower S-shaped turns. Steer that outside foot, knee, and ski into the new turn. You need the speed because round turns slow you down—round turns are great for controlling speed on steeper slopes.

Feel your edges? Most likely you will be using your edges more, both to control and to use the speed to shape those round turns.

Keep up the round turns, steering that outside ski. Once that's comfortable, think of your inside ski: *lighten your inside ski through the turn*. That's right, lighten that inside ski. Don't lift it, just lighten it. What happened? Did it slide alongside your outside ski? Right on! That's a wedge christy! (See illus. 22.)

Some skiers prefer to think of transferring weight to the outside ski rather than lightening the inside one. Try both, and do what works best for you.

DOING A STEM CHRISTY

I remember watching three of Hans Gmoser's helicopter guides descending from the summit plateau of Mount Logan, the highest peak in Canada's Yukon. They were skiing roped together. I watched carefully in hopes of gleaning some off-piste alpine tricks that I could use for our free-heeled descent. To my surprise they were all making controlled stem christies. No parallels, even in the easier snow! Teles sufficed to get us down, but I wanted to know more about using the stem christy in these situations.

If you must control your speed for dicey skiing, the stem christy is an

22
A wedge christy

excellent turn. Advanced skiers use it because the stem produces a quick, controlled-turn initiation—a key to avoiding the sudden acceleration present in the first half of a parallel turn. Stem christies provide excellent side-to-side stability, an indispensable element for negotiating crevasses—especially with a big pack.

As I mentioned earlier, the word **christy** defines a parallel skid with both skis edged in the same direction. **Stem christies** have a stemmed-turn initiation with a weight shift to the outside ski, resulting in a skidded christy or parallel finish.

Try it. From a traverse, stand up tall and stem your outside ski into a wedge position. Stand up as though you want to reach out with that stemming ski. Then step onto it, shifting your weight to the stemmed ski. Steer your ski into the fall line. Sink with your body as you steer through the turn, preparing to stand up for the next stem. Now stem the other ski and *step onto it*. I call this move a **stem-step.** Shift your weight to that stemmed ski. Both skis are then steered parallel into the christy turn finish.

Practice first in a garland, turning only in one direction from a traverse. Unlike when you did your first teles, there's no need to step-turn into the fall line. Let your stem bring you around. Stand up tall and stem-step, then sink and steer your turn around to a stop. Feel the flowing sensation that standing up and sinking produce as you swoop through the fall line.

The next step, linking stem christies, feels quite natural: once you steer your last turn across the fall line, stand tall and stem-step your new outside ski, shifting your weight onto it. With your weight shifted, you're now steering into your next turn (see illus. 23).

23
Linked stem christies

Stand up, sink, stand up, sink—this is an important movement that I will emphasize time and time again throughout this book. It's an unweighting—the sinking lightens your skis. If you don't believe me, try it on your bathroom scale. Stand tall and sink abruptly. Notice how your weight drops when you sink down. Your skis stay lighter, easier to steer, as long as you are sinking.

Here's another exercise: lighten your inside ski as you steer both skis through the fall line. Think "light as a feather" on the inside ski. This gets you steering and turning your outside ski. Your light inside ski will drift parallel to "match" the outside ski—forming that stable parallel christy in your turn finish. Some skiers actually lift their inside ski when they stem-step to exaggerate this lightness (see the last figure in illus. 23).

Now review the three points of focus that will make wedge and stem christies much easier: (1) use plenty of up-and-down movement, starting tall and sinking through the turn; (2) shift your weight onto that stemmed (or wedged) ski; and (3) lighten the inside ski as your skis come through the fall line.

STEERING

By lightening your inside ski in the last exercise you've probably already made some basic parallel turns. The next thing to think about is steering.

As you make wedge or stem christies, think of *steering* your inside ski: *turn it* with your inside foot in the direction of the new turn. That's right. As you lighten your inside ski, actively steer it alongside the outside ski. Move onto the new outside ski, lighten and steer the inside one. Using whichever focal point for steering that best suits your preference, think of pointing your ski, foot, or knee in the direction that you want to go. Are your feet moving together, steering and open-stance parallel?

Try it again. Start with smooth, round, linked stem or wedge christies. Feel the inside ski lighten as you transfer your weight to your outside foot and steer it. Steer the inside foot along with it. You don't need to lift it; as the inside foot lightens, it's easy to steer alongside the outside one (see illus. 24).

MOTION

Now, forget your feet for a minute. Think about motion: standing very tall at the start of the turn as you steer your feet into the fall line, then sinking deeply with your ankles and your knees through the turn. Exaggerate this extension (tall) and flexion (small) so your skis feel light and maneuverable as you start each new turn. Tall, small, tall, small.

Inhale deeply when you stand up and start your turn; exhale as you sink

24
A basic parallel
turn . . . tall, small

through the turn. Inflate to be tall; exhale to be small. Get the feel for this kind of vertical motion and you'll have a fundamental skill that will be with you no matter what technique you choose.

Let's take a break from turning for a minute to practice a few critical skills that are important techniques in themselves and that will help your parallel skiing.

SIDE-SLIPPING

Side-slipping is controlled skidding—releasing your edges and flattening your skis to slide sideways down the hill. Side-slipping isn't just for skill development; it's a technique. Sure, it's an important basic; but a good side-slip is crucial to pressure control in the most advanced skiing. On something steep and narrow I find that, snow allowing, a short side-slip is just what it takes to gain momentum for that difficult first turn.

Practice your side-slip on a short, steep, packed slope.

Note: Take time to tighten your boots. I've often had students who didn't want to hassle with tightening their boots, and they have sacrificed ski and edge control.

Begin by climbing up from the bottom, side-stepping to the top. Are your skis slipping out from under you? If so, then tip them into the hill a little more. Don't lean; just tip the skis, edging with your feet, ankles, and (to a lesser degree) your knees. Once you are partway up the slope, try a downhill side-slip. Face your body downhill: round, relaxed back; stomach in; head up. Then, with your skis across the fall line, let up on your edges, rolling your feet and knees away from the hill. Your skis should side-slip down the hill.

Develop control of your side-slip by alternately flattening your skis and edging them to come to a halt. Try to slide sideways only, with a minimum of forward motion (see illus. 25).

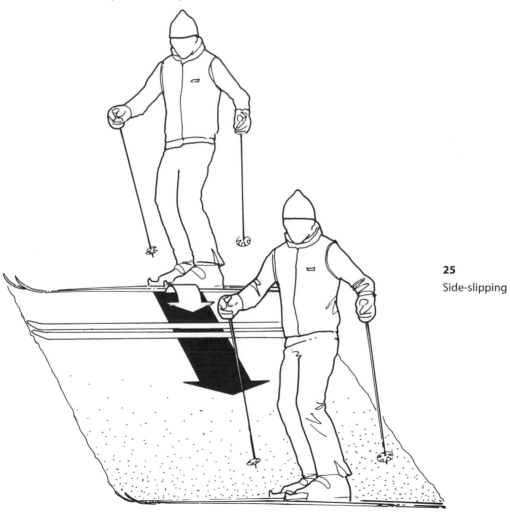

25
Side-slipping

Now try a forward side-slip. This time, forward motion is OK. Start in a slightly downhill traverse. Rise up and roll your knees away from the hill and let your skis side-slip; now sink and roll them into the hill so that they grip and your skis hold the traverse. Experiment with the amount of side-slip so that your skis grip, then slide, then grip, making a wobbly path across the hill.

HERRINGBONE

Herringbone is an alternative climbing technique to the side-step that you practiced in the last exercise. It's what I would call a "short-term climbing technique"—something that you will use for short distances. Because of its foot-splayed position, it's used in place of the side-step on gentler slopes. It is, essentially, walking duck-footed up the hill (see illus. 26).

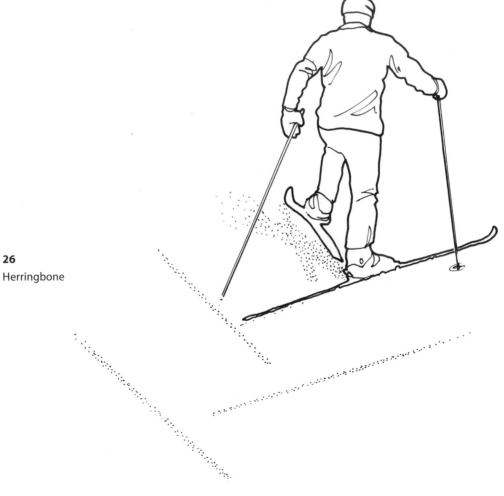

26
Herringbone

Make a wedge, backwards: with your tips spread, tails together, step uphill from inside edge to inside edge. Press the insides of your feet into the hill to gain more edge. Try it with less edge, then more edge, to get a feel for how much edge it requires to grip on your slope.

A SET OF GARLANDS

The last two exercises focused on edge control. Now we'll build on those exercises and try a set of garlands. We'll make a series of parallel stop-turns, progressively beginning each turn more in the fall line.

Start by picking a shallow traversing line and turn uphill to a stop. Weight and steer your outside ski away from the fall line, and at the same time, *lighten and steer the inside one.* Feel the skis "match," parallel?

As your confidence grows, step into the fall line a little more each time you begin a new stop-turn. Each turn starts with less traverse, until finally there is no traverse at all. Once you are comfortable turning without a traverse, step directly down the hill, beginning the stop-turn in the fall line. Don't forget the vertical motion. Sometimes I think of this movement as "sink and steer, rise, sink and steer."

A note about your feet: be sure to keep them hip-width—no narrower (refer back to illus. 24). Don't worry if you feel a bit wobbly. With practice you will soon feel more solid. Practicing hockey stops (the next exercise) will help solidify your two-footed steering—steering not only your weighted outside foot into the turn, but your lighter inside foot in the same direction. Hockey stops are a very abrupt version of a parallel turn with lots of skid. As you temper, or soften, those abrupt movements, your parallels will get more carvy and elegant.

HOCKEY STOPS

You need a good emergency stop. The **hockey stop** is the quintessential slamming on the brakes. Learn it well.

A hockey stop isn't just for stopping. Practice it and you'll develop greater maneuverability and control for your parallel turns. Its abrupt two-footed steering/twisting and resultant two-footed skid are just overexaggerated versions of the two-footed steering and christy of the basic parallel turn.

Work on hockey stops on a smooth slope. Standing tall, point your skis straight down the hill in a wide, stable stance. Push off for speed. Once you gain momentum, sink abruptly, flexing at the ankles and knees (not at the waist!) and steer (twist) your skis hard across the fall line. Continue facing down the hill as your skis come across the slope. Your parallel skis will skid you to a stop (see illus. 27).

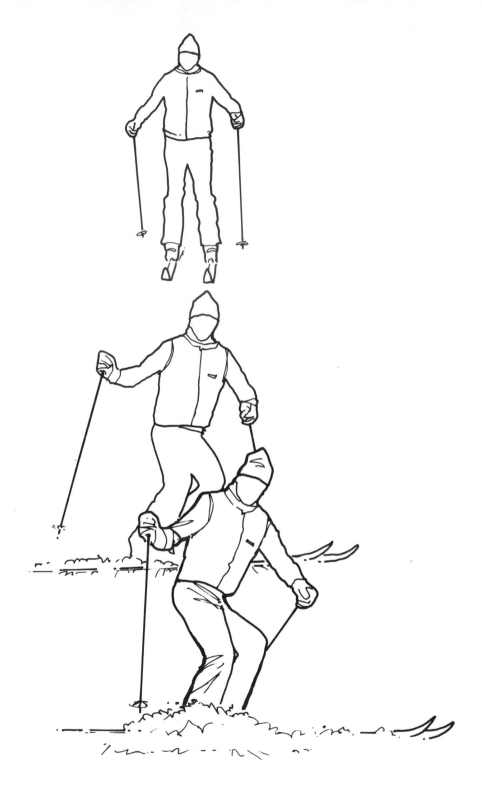

27
A hockey stop

Do lots of hockey stops in both directions so that you are comfortable stopping on either side. Remember, this is your emergency stop. One note of warning: practice it below obstacles—or your friends—to avoid dangerous collisions. I've seen too many skiers try to stop above a group of waiting friends and instead wipe them all out.

FLEXION AND EXTENSION

When I refer to up-and-down movement, or vertical motion, I often put the phrase in quotes. That's because flexion and extension of your legs really doesn't create a purely up-and-down motion. I'm not trying to get you popping straight up and down like toast out of the toaster. Rather, the angle of the hill makes the movement of your body fall somewhere between up-and-down and in-and-out. It's an overall flexion and extension motion of your body. I can't emphasize this motion too much.

Try making some turns with lots of flexion and extension—tall, small, tall, small. Then make some turns with no movement at all. Which do you prefer? In all downhill techniques, flexion and extension movements are what make the skis work for you. They allow you to control and use the pressures that gravity and centrifugal force create against your edges. They are the key to more carve and less skid (refer back to illus. 23 and 24).

There are many more tips in the Advanced Skills section devoted specifically to these kinds of movements. The point is to develop a *three-dimensional motion* in your skiing—a flowing down the hill while your body moves dynamically into the fall line, extending and flexing, in and out. Stick with it. Move all of the time. Stay away from "positions"; be alive as you ski.

The Haute Route

~

We barely bridged the icy glacial stream, popped off our skis, and stumbled up the moraine. Up a steep incline was a closed ski trail covered in ice, year-old cow shit, and pine cones. Perfect. We might not have to walk. This icy minefield dropped us in the village of Furi. An open outdoor stube shimmered like a mirage, an oasis. Behind it was the téleferique that dropped steeply to Zermatt.

Beer, beautiful beer.

We dumped our packs on the grass and ordered a round. My French friends and I were giddy, sipping pressions from huge steins; tired, elated, and crinkly from sun and sweat. Our conversation was comical. My Italian companion had bailed in Arolla with sore feet and would meet us in Zermatt for the Monte Rosa. Without Marco's pidgin French, our communication was reduced to my speaking slowly in Italian and waving my arms, my friends replying slowly in French and waving their arms, and all of us wondering if Romance languages were really so similar.

That was an excerpt from the diary that I kept on the Haute Route. Chamonix–Zermatt–Saas Fee makes up the Haute Route, the best-known ski mountaineering route in Europe. Its setting is breathtaking and, in spite of today's touristy popularity, it is the *haute route*—the first established high ski traverse through the Alps and still considered one of the best lines. Compared with other routes, the Haute Route is crowded, with mediocre huts and pathetic Swiss and French beer. Still, it's classic—even though there are numerous longer, more remote routes closer to Bavarian taps.

This "classic" Haute Route (there are numerous variants) evolved with the early exploration of its individual high peaks and passes in the Swiss and French Alps. The peaks and passes were linked together in 1861 by a French-guided group of British, who named it the High-level Road—translated into French as Haute Route. It might seem strange that this famous route was pioneered by the Brits, but they were some of the keenest pioneers of skiing and general alpine exploration. In traditional European style, they hired local guides as part of their party. It's thought that, as late as the mid-1950s, no unguided British parties had completed the Haute Route.

Today the Haute Route passes through a number of modern alpine resorts. Tourers can make use of lifts and *téleferiques* (cable cars) to get to snowline, avoiding unnecessary climbs and adding to the downhill skiing. One can get used to that custom very quickly.

The skiing on the Haute Route, unless you take certain detours, need not be difficult. I remember one friend who briefed me for the trip saying that the skiing was dead-easy: "With a strong snowplow and controlled side-slip anyone could do the route." In retrospect, I would agree that one could *do* it, but it would be a shame to miss some of the exciting detours and smooth, steep, beautiful corn slopes. And, if all you had was a wedge and a side-slip in your repertoire, you'd probably find yourself scared silly wedging down some exposed arête with a village at your feet—thousands of feet below.

This style of skiing, when compared with normal piste and off-piste lift skiing, is like alpine climbing as compared with sport climbing: ski mountaineering requires many skills beyond the perfect turn. In fact, you don't need the perfect turn. It's more

© Paul Parker

important to have survival skiing skills in all conditions.

Skiing in Europe is different. If it's wilderness that you are after, Europe isn't the place to tour. It's expensive; *téleferiques* are often visible from remote places; routes can be crowded; and huts prevail. But given the mountains, the incredible hut systems, and the support of an established ski mountaineering "culture," it's easy to take the disadvantages in stride. Any skier who has stood on top of one of the big peaks like the Jungfrau, the Monte Rosa, or Mont Blanc is already planning the next trip.

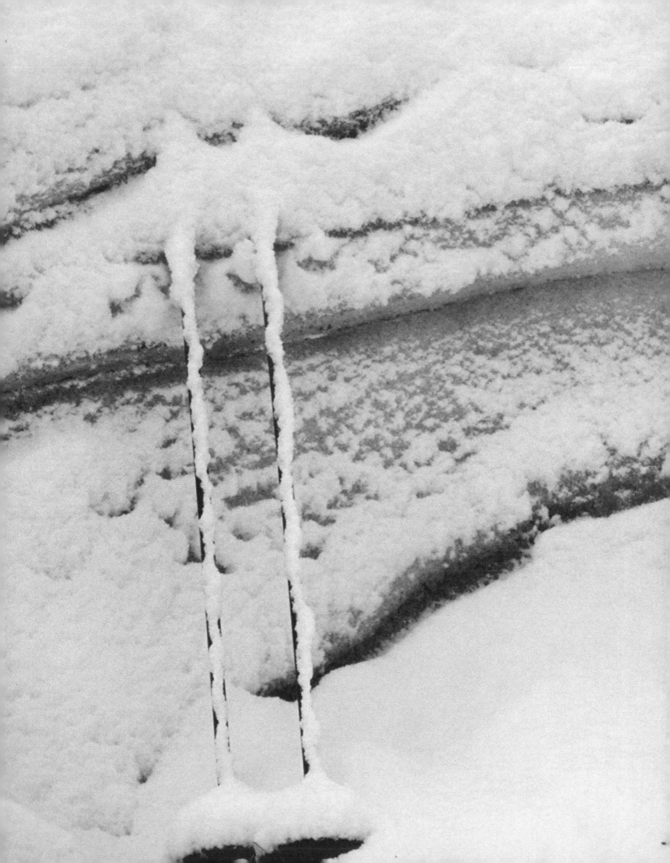

MAINTENANCE

Free-heel Ski Care

Caring for your skis properly makes a huge difference in their performance. Whether you find it therapeutic to tune them yourself, or you'd rather pay a shop to get them buffed, keeping your skis in shape will make them—and you—feel better every time you ski.

TUNING NEW SKIS

The first thing I do with a new pair of skis is take them to my favorite local tuning shop to get them stone-ground, tuned, and waxed. "The full deal" we call it. Certainly it's an additional cost, but I highly recommend this practice with *any* brand of ski, no matter how they are prepared at the factory. If the shop where you bought the skis has the capability, and they're good with their machines, ask them to throw in the service. If that's not an option, ask around for the best tuning shop.

My criteria for a ski tune is that it is predictable and easy-skiing so that I can get the most out of the skis and my technique. I ask for "a 1-degree base and side-edge bevel, tip to tail, with slight de-tuning of the tips and tails." You can carry a stone or piece of emery paper to further de-tune the tips and tails if desired.

Photo on pages 78–79
© Ace Kvale

While we expect that kind of precision, we must remember that both grinders and their operators are not created equal. Ask around; see where the local hotshots and alpine racers go before you relinquish your skis to someone's machines.

Why spend the bucks? No matter how well they're tuned in the factory, skis change during transportation and changes in climate. Skis are often built in the summer months when it's hot and humid, and are then transported to cold, dry, high-altitude climates. Layers within the ski are very different materials that cure and change differently. Skis are usually transported with

Photo on preceding page
© John Norris

protective base and edge coatings that should be removed. And base materials dry out and contract when curing and in transportation, and can contract further the first time you put them on cold snow.

New skis need to be tuned. It will make the difference between having to deal with an unnecessary challenge, or enjoying that precise, effortless bliss of a new pair of boards.

Start with a Flat Base

A ski's base should be flat. If part of the base is high or low, you'll feel it. High-based (convex) skis are squirrely and nervous, especially when running straight on those high bases instead of tipped up on their edges. "Railed" skis—concave—have edges higher than their bases, and can be especially desperate in transition from turn to turn. As though on rails, railed skis don't want to change direction: they're difficult to get up onto their edge, and are especially difficult to release that edge into a new turn. Either of these problems diminishes the performance of your new skis, but railed skis are especially hard to manage.

To determine if your bases are flat, first check them with a true bar—a metal bar machined perfectly flat for eyeballing bases and edges (see illus. 28). Hold the ski up to the light and move the true bar down the full length

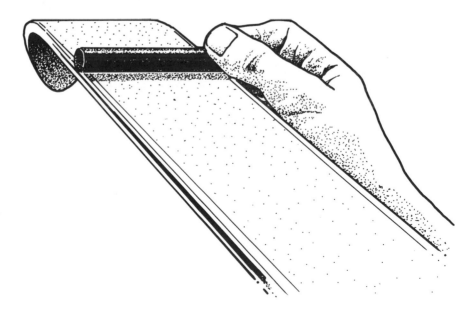

28
Checking for a flat
base with a true bar

of the ski, looking for daylight between the ski base and the bar. Light will show where the base or the metal edges are low. No light will show through spots that are flat or too high. High bases should be scraped or ground down; skis with high edges should be filed flat.

A shop can make quick work of a high or low base, but if the convenience of a stone grinder isn't available, you can scrape base-high skis with a metal scraper until they are flat, or flat-file railed skis to reduce their concavity. To flatten a high base, hold your ski securely in ski vises—also support the ski in the middle—and scrape the high spots down with the sharp side of a metal scraper. Tip the scraper away from you and push it using long, even strokes from tip to tail (see illus. 29). (You can sharpen a dull scraper with a file,

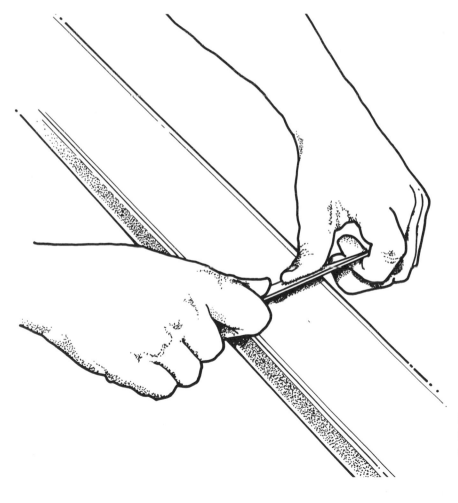

29
Flattening a high base
with a metal scraper

taking care to keep the scraper edge flat.) Be careful not to flex the scraper—I like to hold a plastic scraper behind my metal one to help keep it flat. You should be able to feel it grip those areas of the ski base that are too high. Check the ski base frequently to be sure you aren't removing too much base material. Scrape until the material is perfectly flat and flush with the ski edge. Take your time.

Flat Filing

On a railed ski, light will show between the base and the true bar, but none will show between the edges and the bar. The more shape, the harder it is to ski a railed ski. If the bases aren't too concave, flat filing can solve the problem. If the bases are very concave, which is common with new skis in the modern monocoque/cap construction, you should get the skis machine-ground.

For heavy flat filing, use at least a 10-inch mill bastard file. Some prefer an auto body file or a Panser, but with these aggressive tools you must know when to stop. It's a lot easier to take off material than put it back. Whichever file you choose, grip it close to the ski, placing your thumbs over the ski's edges (see illus. 30). Be careful not to bend the file when you grip it; keep it flat. Place it on the ski at an angle so that its teeth cut. You will soon get the feel of the best angle according to the design of your file. You can push or pull the file, whichever seems most comfortable; but the file's tang should always point away from the cutting direction.

File with long, smooth strokes. Clean the file often with the brush side of a file card; the metal side dulls files and is best saved for hard-to-remove wax residue and plastic filings. Keep the base of the ski free of filings with a rag or brush. File the edges until they are flush with the base, checking the ski frequently with a true bar.

Beveling the Edge

A beveled edge—tuning the ski with its edges inclined slightly so that they are lower than the level of the plastic base—makes your skis smoother and easier to use. Beveling lowers the grabby edge, making the ski easier to initiate—especially important with the "edginess" of shaped skis. Beveling also minimizes that "too sharp" sensation in soft and crusty snow and on steep slopes. Experts use bevel to allow them to ski their boards farther away from their body for more edge on steeper slopes and at higher speeds.

Once again, as outlined above, the easiest route is to take your skis to a well-equipped shop to be stone-ground and edge-beveled precisely to your

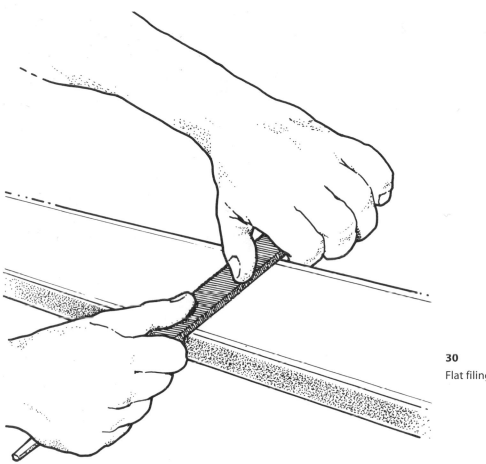

instructions. And again, when giving these instructions, my "all-around" preference is a 1-degree base-edge and side-edge bevel, tip to tail. This is a good rule of thumb to start from—those who prefer something different should already know it.

If you don't have the heavy machinery to do it, you have some simple options. The most foolproof tool for edge beveling at home is a quality hand beveler. If you don't care to buy yet another tool, you can do an effective base-edge bevel with a piece of duct tape on a 10-inch file. Side-beveling is a bit tougher—it's hard to be precise when you're working with such a narrow surface. If you don't have an edge-beveling tool that works with the side edge, I'd bevel the base edge, sharpen the side edges, and leave it at that.

If you do buy a hand beveler, try to find one that can bevel both the base edge and the side edge—many of them only bevel the side edge. Follow the instructions included with your tool for both procedures, base-edge and side-edge beveling, set at 1 degree.

To bevel with a file and duct tape, carefully wrap the end of your 10-inch or 12-inch file with two wraps of the tape (see illus. 31). Rub the tape flat, making sure there are no raw edges or wrinkles. Place the file on the ski with the tape over one edge, the file over the other edge. The tape will lift one side of the file so that it tunes the opposite edge with a slight bevel. File with

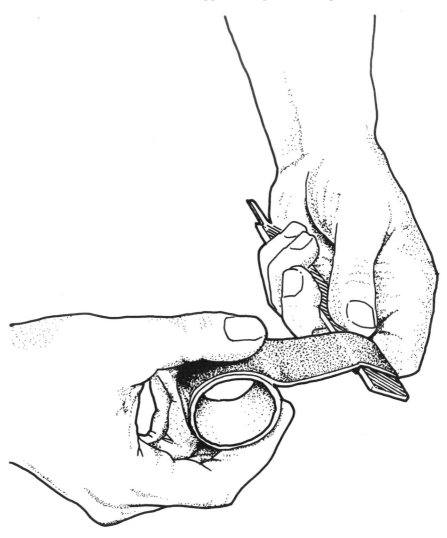

31
Taping your file for beveling your edges

long, smooth strokes, just as you did when you were flat filing. You can monitor your edge bevel by the new metal that is exposed as you file; or, if you're not sure of yourself, use a side-filing trick: color the edge with a felt-tipped marker before filing. Be careful to keep the ink off of your plastic base. File until the ink is gone and the full width of the edge is beveled. It's also best to extend the bevel into the base for about an edge-width. Now turn the file around and repeat the process on the other edge.

By taping your file carefully and replacing the tape if it packs too flat, you can do an excellent job using this method. You'll quickly get the feel of your files and how much they are cutting. Take your time and use your true bar. If you remove too much metal you'll have to scrape the base down and start all over.

Side Filing

When you hit a rock, a ski's metal edge is work-hardened by the impact. The result is a rough spot called a **burr,** and its surface is usually much harder than the rest of the edge. You may have the same problem with a new ski whose edges have been work-hardened by the manufacturer's final base grinding. With work-hardened edges you can file until you're blue in the face, but you'll make little progress.

First you want to get rid of these hard spots. Put one of your skis firmly in a vise, and go over any work-hardened areas with a stone. This extra step will minimize wear on yourself and your files, reducing the hard spot so that your file will bite.

Next, side-file the edge to restore it to 90 degrees, and to smooth any nicks or burrs. If you use a shorter, more flexible file, hold the file in the palm of your hand and run it lengthwise along the side edge in long, smooth strokes (see illus. 32). Be sure to keep the file flat against the edge. If you've got a bigger, more rigid file, you can hold it in both hands at an angle to the edge as though you are flat-filing. You will need to keep your thumbs pressed right over the edge to keep from bending the file. It is important to file evenly and perpendicular to the ski base. If the new metal is exposed evenly along the full width of the edge, you are doing fine. This is a great place for the felt-tipped marker trick: color the side edge and then file the ink off evenly.

After sharpening your edges you should remove the burr created by the file and then dull the edges back from the tips and tails. The too-sharp burr will hang up the skis in turns, and the skis will behave as though they were railed. I prefer a burr stick for removing the burr. A **burr stick** is a "rubber

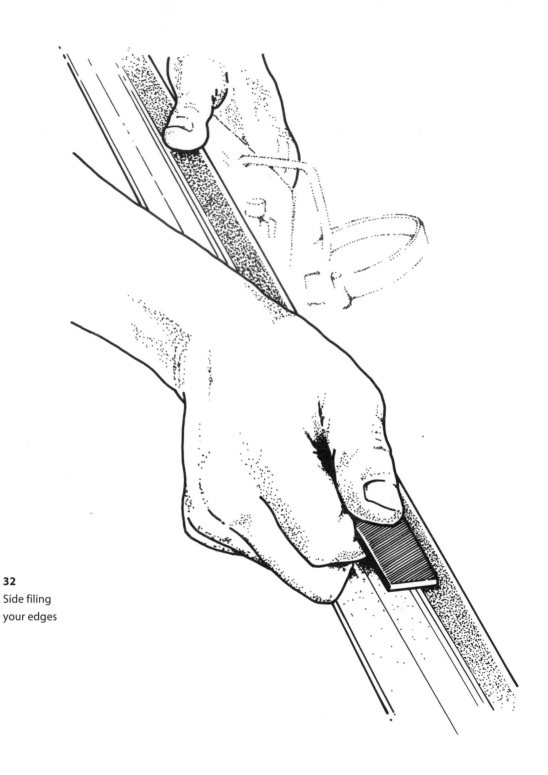

32
Side filing
your edges

stone," like an eraser with just the right amount of abrasiveness to remove the burr without losing the keen edge.

DE-TUNING YOUR SKIS

Whether tuned in the shop or by hand, you want to be sure that your skis are de-tuned slightly. If you have a burr stick, run it along the edges tip-to-tail. If you don't, lightly run a fine whetstone or emery paper the full length of the edge at a 45-degree angle to the ski base. Then use your burr stick or stone to dull the edges back 10 to 15 centimeters from the contact surface of each ski's tip and tail. It is a good idea to carry some emery paper or a small pocket stone. Diamond stones are great for this application. Depending on the snow, you might want to "de-tune" your skis' edges a bit more if they seem catchy.

Once your skis have been properly tuned you will never want to go back to an untuned ski. To keep them at their best, occasionally touch them up with your stone or a light side filing. Keep them sharp, especially underfoot. And stay out of the rocks.

WAXING

A multitude of waxes are available, with very different chemistries and uses. For the free-heel backcountry and downhill skier, this multitude can be lumped into two general categories: **kick wax** and **glide wax.**

Kick Wax

Cross-country kick wax grips the snow—or, in fact, the snow grips it—by **crystalline bonding.** It works like magic, gripping when you push down, gliding when you push forward. When you push down, the snow crystals stick into the wax, giving you purchase. Colder, dryer snow crystals are sharper and better defined. Colder waxes are harder because these sharper crystals have greater grip and will stick in the wax if it's too soft. Warmer crystals are more rounded—and wetter—so the wax must be softer for the crystals to grip, and a softer wax will slide against these rounded crystals. Refrozen crystals are not only round and wet, but abrasive, so klister must be softer and very abrasion-resistant—long-lasting on your skis (and gloves and pants).

The use of wax for propulsion in the backcountry has changed as free-heel gear has gotten heavier and more downhill-oriented. Not long ago, most edged backcountry skis had at least a camber and a half and skiers used kick wax as their primary means of forward purchase. Skins were saved for only the steepest climbs. Today the reverse is true. Most skis have alpine single-camber, and skiers commonly use skins as their primary means of grip, with a can or two of wax in their packs for long, flat sections.

Unless your tours are primarily straight up and straight down, it still makes sense to carry a little wax. Most wax manufacturers offer a two-wax system—one wax for wet snow and one for dry. This system is the simplest, easiest choice for occasional waxing.

For nordic skis, most widely used cross-country kick waxes are based on a color-coded system that's organized according to temperature. With this system you'll get the broadest range of options. Today many of the color-coded waxes have fancy new names, but most manufacturers still color-code the cans. You can make your own two-wax system with a couple of cans of these color-coded waxes, selecting the colors according to the season. In very cold winter I might choose a green or blue (cold) and a purple (around freezing); in warmer conditions I'd go with purple (around freezing) and red or yellow (above freezing).

"Crayon" the chosen wax on the ski in the kick zone. The length of the zone depends on your ski's camber, but start from your heel forward for about 50 centimeters (2 feet). If your skis slip, you can go longer. Using colder waxes (below freezing) you can be a bit more generous and wax longer, but when using softer, warmer waxes, it's best to be conservative and stick to about 50 centimeters. Smooth the wax by rubbing it briskly with a synthetic cork.

Once your skis are waxed, start up the trail and test your wax job. If it works, don't fix it. If it slips, lengthen the "kicker" toward the tip and tail. If it still slips, add more layers, smoothing each one with a cork. Several smooth, thin layers are more effective than one thick one. And if it still slips, switch to a softer wax, starting with a smooth, thin layer again. As you go softer, start shorter, waxing the middle of the ski first (2 to 3 feet) and then lengthening the kick if you continue to slip.

Glide Wax

Glide wax is a harder wax of a composition designed to glide. It nourishes skis' polyethylene bases and makes them glide and turn more easily. It is also temperature-matched for the highest performance and is usually applied with a hot iron and then scraped to a thin film. It's important to glide-wax your skis as often as possible. Many skiers think it makes their skis too fast and hard to control, but in fact glide-waxing makes them turn more easily so that you can better control your speed.

To hot-wax your skis at home, use a dry (not steam) iron set on medium heat. Hold the wax against the iron and drip it onto the ski. (If the wax smokes, the iron is too hot.) Then iron the wax into the ski, being sure to keep the iron moving to prevent damage to the base of the ski. After the wax has cooled, scrape it with a sharp plastic scraper. In cold temperatures the wax should be almost invisible. For warm conditions the wax can be a little thicker, but it should still be scraped thoroughly.

You can glide-wax on the trail, using an easy-to-apply universal glider like Notwax or F4. This kind of glide-waxing can be especially helpful to keep sliding on long tours or when the snow is in rapid transition. Be sure that the glider you choose is compatible with adhesive skins.

You can also rub hard glider on a ski like kick wax and then cork it smooth. This method is not as durable as ironing or the liquid/paste universal waxes, but is quite effective when hard wax is all you have and an electric outlet isn't available.

SKINS

Today, skins dominate as a means of backcountry propulsion. Originally called "sealskins" (that's what they were made from), skins provide purchase for straight climbing where waxed or waxless skis would require herringbone or side-step.

Can you travel only with skins? For straight-up, straight-down tours I just carry skins; but for longer tours that involve long flat sections, I carry both skins and a simple wax kit as I've described above. Skins grip like Velcro but don't have wax's glide. If your tour involves a lot of flat terrain, even if it's on heavy tele or randonnée gear, a can of wax can save energy. For more information on climbing skins, see the Free-heel Equipment chapter.

Anything Goes

~

Less than a half-hour's hike brought us to the 13,000-foot summit. The view was stunning: from the Maroon Bells, to Pike's Peak, to the backside of Long's. We pushed off Peak 8's north side, hop-turned through the steep *sastrugi*, and headed for a hole in the cornice that the patrol had blasted off. Below were two sets of tight arcs cut through the deep, wind-deposited powder.

It was one of those spring days that you remember: calm, bluebird, one day after the last storm. I was free-heel skiing at Breckenridge with a group of old buddies: Allan Bard, John Dostal, and John Tidd.

"What's all that black stuff on the snow?" asked Dostal, scrutinizing the two patrollers' tracks.

"Powder burns from this morning's control route."

"Hmmm . . . Don't see much gunpowder on the slopes in Vermont," said Tidd.

I dropped in first, opting for short-radius alpine turns, avoiding a couple of deep bomb holes. I expected the other boys to make some teles, but no one wanted to change the radius—everyone made fall-line alpine turns down the steep pitch.

After twenty-five or thirty turns the skiing turned to breakable crust. We each fell back on our best survival strategy: telemark, parallel, or a combination of the two. Most chose half and half. We continued down the lower bowl, cutting up the seamless surface. A traverse brought us to our ride for another lap.

When these old cronies had showed up on my doorstep that morning, I'd figured I would finally find the answer to a question—and assignment—that had been nagging me for weeks. "Is there a *right* way to telemark?" my friend at *Powder* had asked. The more I'd thought about it, the more confused I felt. Certainly the beginnings of telemark *I'd* experienced were like those of snowboarding: an alternative, a rebellion. Whatever works, go for it. So I turned to my buddies, all veterans of the early days, old-time skiers and instructors. They could help me with the answer.

Photo on preceding page

© Ace Kvale

Even as we put on our boots and organized our skis, it was obvious there weren't many rules for these guys. I had thought that there would be some leather-boot hold-outs, but everyone's boots were plastic. And the skis—the skimpy ones were only a *little* wider than the new-wave alpine GS skis designed for big turns. The others were *way* wider: a pair of 180-centimeter-wide randonnée skis, and a pair of "chubbies." Not very traditional hardware for a neo-traditionalist sport.

As soon as the upper lift was opened we hitched a ride and traversed off-piste. With the first turns down the steep bowl, it was obvious the wind and sun had already had their effect. The skiing was difficult. We found a few soft pockets, but they were connected by steep, smooth, seamless breakable crust, with no warning of a change from turn to turn. I thought to myself how much I like this kind of skiing, but when hosting visitors, I usually don't seek it out. Yet realizing that the conditions weren't dampening anyone's enthusiasm, I knew it would be a memorable day. We had the whole place to ourselves.

Our group of four had a lot of history. In the past fifteen years we'd been in the same ski schools, two of us were on the PSIA Demo Team together, we'd snow-cat skied, and we'd skied the Sierra Crest.

John Tidd was a member of the PSIA Nordic Team and director/owner of Mountain Meadows Ski Touring Center. He sold his nordic area, using what he'd learned about snow farming to start his business building cross-country groomers and tracksetters. Tidd has always been an agile telemark skier, using that turn to exhaustion. In bumps,

powder, and junk, *that's his turn*. He's pretty analytical about it.

John Dostal is a well-known ski adventurer and writer, and co-author of the entertaining nordic classic *Cross-country Skiing*. Dostal's thoughtful, wry wit permeates everything he does, including his writing for many of the major ski and outdoor magazines. Dostal is an evangelist, spreading the gospel of free-heel skiing.

Allan Bard—"Bardini"—is a legend. A dedicated ski and climbing guide in the High Sierra, Allan was committed to developing guiding as the profession it deserves to be. He was a gifted writer, speaker, and one of California's earliest free-heel explorers. Bard pioneered many new ski routes on free-heel gear, including the "Red Line Traverse," the Haute Route of the Sierra. Bard couldn't *not* be funny: always entertaining, a great storyteller, keeping us all spellbound with his humor and his very pure philosophy of life. The summer after this memorable ski day, Allan fell to his death while guiding in the Tetons. Bardini lives on . . .

Figuring the crust might be more malleable on a sunnier exposure, we next chose an east-facing line. In the direct sun on this unseasonably warm early morning, the snow had already metamorphosed from frozen coral to manky, ski-sucking junk. It was a free-for-all; everybody tried everything. Dostal and Bard made mostly parallels with the odd telemark. Bard threw in a couple of unplanned royal christies in one especially unconsolidated section. Tidd followed suit and started with parallels, launched over the handlebars, rolled, and changed his tune to teles without missing a beat. The most effective move that I could find was a leap-parallel turn, using the steepness to leap (more like *hurling* myself) into the fall line, landing on both feet and arcing out of it—Hurl Turns.

Remembering my mission, I questioned my friends on the lift rides. Bard was first. I asked him what he thought of the current state of telemarking.

"Telemarking *is not a sport*, it's a *turn*, just a turn . . . just another in a repertoire of many turns. As nords we can make any turn we want. We can even make a passable snowboard turn, if pressed. I choose the kind of turn I make according to what the snow demands."

The next run was a different exposure, one less hammered by the sun. Skis came off for a short hike, the trail broken with one patroller's bootprints. No one else was up here for recreation.

I picked the steepest line because it was easiest to get airborne, freeing the feet from the sucking action of the crusty surface. I used both teles and parallels, trying to stay compact in either technique. A "tight" stance was best because I wanted my feet close and collected *under* me when I landed and punched through the crust—not too spread out either fore-to-aft or side-to-side. Bard and Dostal were next with mostly alpine turns, equally determined to stay compact. Tidd went for it with teles. Watching him from below, we applauded his agility. We took a break and I got Tidd's opinion on turns.

"For me, tele skiing in that situation (if I put the energy into it) feels more secure and stable to handle variations in the snow. But I pay the price using that much muscle power. In parallel, especially if you stand taller, you are using your skeleton to pressure the skis. In tele, your thighs bear the pressure."

Obviously there was a consensus in our group that telemark isn't the only kind of free-heel turn. In certain kinds of snow, like the day's crusty conditions, many skiers prefer parallels. But that wasn't my quandary—parallel turns are well-defined. I wanted to know what they thought about the more eclectic of turns, the *telemark*. Tidd, very technical, and a tele skier through and through, could shed some light on his feelings about the right and wrong way to make the telemark.

"The low stance works for some people; high stance works for others. I see a lot of tele skiers jumping, turning their skis with the transition in the air, landing in a tele that's turned all the way across the hill. It's not at all elegant. But it works."

Skating a gentle uphill traverse brought us to a steep line through some wind- and avalanche-flagged *krumholz*. The tenacious little shrubs were the only features on the wind-fat pitch. The first half was perfect wind-board: firm with an edgeable surface, like felt. There was a hollow sound just as the snow went breakable—fair warning to get your feet clear for the start of your next turn. We all instinctively telemarked when the snow changed, our best defense against a sudden launch over the tips.

Dostal entertained me on the lift ride.

"I like skiing with good skiers, watching them. So much of skiing is knowing how to watch and learn. 'The rising tide lifts all boats,' so to speak. I saw how you jump-turn, realizing that, parallel or tele, you don't jump your skis *across* the fall line, but you jump *into* the fall line to clear the snow, and then arc out of it. That's something I noticed and will take home with me. Not some final form.

"What's cool about telemarking is that we're discussing a kind of *freedom*. You read the alpine magazines and they often discuss a kind of form that's useless for skiing backcountry snow. Not to say that many instructors aren't excellent skiers, but much of the teaching technique on the groomed snow isn't what works for our kind of skiing. It's like Bard says: 'you have to *do it*, get *in* it.'"

We "did it" until the bell rang, with only a brief lunch break to ponder my notes and compare strategies. The difficult, unpredictable skiing continued in the afternoon until the upper lifts closed, leaving us no choice but to ski perfect, corn-topped corduroy the rest of the day. It was so easy. Bard, ever philosophical, set us straight on our last quad chair ride.

"What we did today was the classic case of looking down something and thinking 'this looks like absolute shit.' Then skiing it— all agreeing that it wasn't so bad. It's an attitude. The roots of telemark are an attitude of adventure, 'confronting the unknown' with what were once seen as inferior tools. For me, that's the right way to ski. Not a final form."

Dostal added, "The funny thing is, in all of this discussion about technique, *none of us*—including the Norwegians, with all of their telemark history—skis the way we did twenty years ago. It looks completely different. Every now and then you still see throwbacks with wool hats, hands in the air

and their back ski stuck into the front instep trying to turn a pair of stiff, skinny racing skis. Miserable. But that's not what most people are doing anymore. Now it's much more free-form.

"We could probably all agree there are more wrong ways to telemark than there are right ways. There are a number of real mistakes, but in terms of final form, you can't go wrong by *keeping your feet moving*. I see these skiers sticking to the telemark 'position,' doing the Sondre 'position' until they fall over.

"Keep it moving."

Back home, thirsts quenched and plans laid for a future ski trip, my friends had to take off for a dinner engagement at Copper. I reviewed my notes—I wanted to get some of this down while it was fresh on my mind.

It was obvious from my own reflections and my buddies' opinions that we all react strongly against rules—even the *idea* of rules. Yet realistically, it's not like there are *no* rules. In fact there are many classic mistakes that one tries to avoid. Today's "proper" technique has developed both through an evolution and specialization, sometimes— but not always—eclipsing older styles of skiing.

Technique evolves with what is possible. When judged by today's standards our free-heel technique twenty years ago was rudimentary—even wrong—due in part to our skis being much skinnier and our boots much lower. Skiers *needed* the telemark because its low, genuflected position kept their centers of gravity low and gave fore-to-aft stability, even on the lightest of gear. Those telemarks, low and steered, were very different from more modern arcs. Today teles are taller, using the leverage of tall boots to bend the skis and carve the turns.

Parallel turns were very difficult except in the best conditions. Most of us didn't have an alpine background, and avoided both the technique and its alpine fundamentals. It wasn't telemark dogma.

Dogma's changed; these fundamentals have become necessity as we have ventured onto the same terrain as alpine skiers. Tele or parallel, we now focus on key points like facing down the fall line, anticipating the next turn, clean pole plants, rebound, and crisp, carved turns. Better gear helps us do that. We've refined our teles and parallel turns because we *can*.

Look at poling, for example. We don't need poles as outriggers like those cliché tele photos. We can use our poles just for timing, avoiding the old-style double pole plants that "square" us to our skis. In the old days square, and rotated, was the only way that we could keep from launching over the bow. Today too square is just a hindrance, a very static posture making your turns hard to bring around.

Technique becomes more specialized. Tele skiers are making choices in the kind of skiing that they do, and developing specialized techniques for it. I recently skied in Lillehammer with a couple of Norwegian racers. The snow was bulletproof, and they were making their turns race-style, with all the weight and pressure on their front ski. Watching from below, with my hand I could block out the back leg from their profile and their bodies were in an alpine racing posture—nothing resembling what we've coined as a telemark. Yet they were tele-marking. They showed me their experimental asymmetric skis that had much less sidecut on the uphill edge—the edge that is key to using your back ski. And these guys ripped. Their specialized approach—a very effective one on-piste—was developed for gates.

For all-mountain skiing that approach is a disaster. We don't delete the back ski, we *emphasize* it. That back ski gets weight, edge, and pressure in a stable two-footed tech-nique. None of us is wrong; these divergent techniques have evolved as what's best for the task. We're free to choose.

A few years ago Andy Dappen wrote an "Opinion" in *Powder* called "Why Telemark? Is Pinning Losing the Weighting Game to Slimmed-down Randonnée Gear?" When I first read it I felt a bit embarrassed being a "telemark" skier—I ski randonnée, too, and clearly understand Andy's arguments for randonnée gear over tele.

Yet after taking a hard look at the sport, and trying to answer this complicated question of a *right* way to do it, I realized that it's easy to miss the point, thinking that lighter-weight gear is the reason to telemark. Weight is secondary. So is making a *certain* kind of telemark. What's more important is *freedom*; both the mobility to get away from snow that's been disturbed by man, and the freedom to make a decent version of the telemark—or whatever kind of turn you choose—without worrying about a final form.

Free heels. Anything *still* goes. It's all about freedom, not final form.

Training

Ilike to stay fit because I feel better. It makes skiing and summer activities more fun. For me, everyday exercise is a necessity, like eating and sleeping. That's the spirit of this chapter. We'll be talking about staying fit for better turns and for enjoyment of backcountry skiing—not competitive skiing. If you're competing, I'd recommend a qualified coach and a scientific training schedule to remain injury-free and to obtain your best results.

The best training for skiing is skiing, but we all don't have the luxury of skiing year-round. Besides, you need to participate in exercise other than skiing to develop the muscles that aren't so important to turns but that just might stave off fatigue and injury while skiing. And your head needs a break. It's great to enjoy the variety of other activities.

The first criterion for any kind of training is to choose a form of exercise that you enjoy enough to maintain. If you don't like it, you probably won't do it. Another criterion—one to be approached prudently—is specificity. If you have to make maximum use of a limited amount of training time, muscle-specific exercises will produce the greatest benefit. World-class coaches emphasize this training specificity to the extreme because they want their athletes to make the most of every training minute. The danger of being too specific is that it can be more like work. I try to choose an exercise first because it's fun, and second because it's applicable to skiing.

STRETCHING

First, always start with an easy warm-up before you stretch. This is crucial, since cold muscles aren't very elastic. Start easy to get your pulse up and your blood moving. Warm down in the same way, slowing to relax your muscles. Don't cool off too quickly.

Stretching before a workout is a great psyche-up and helps to prevent

Photo on preceding page
© Scott Cramer

muscle injury. Read up on the subject, and establish a routine for major muscle groups. Bob Anderson's *Stretching* is a classic, an excellent primer. Be sensitive to your body: if a muscle or muscle group feels tight or fatigued, it could probably use some gentle stretching.

ORGANIZING AN EXERCISE SCHEDULE

The more you exercise, the more important it is to rest. Organize your schedule to include both hard and easy days for maximum benefit from your training. Alternate the hard and easy days, and take one complete rest day each week. Otherwise you will become tired and overtrained. You need to stay rested to get the most enjoyment from each workout.

How long should you exercise each day? You don't have to maintain a rigid schedule to get plenty of positive benefit from training, but some guidelines are helpful. These days coaches acknowledge that quality is more important than quantity. Using a "normal" week as an example, I exercise about an hour each workday, reserve a long, easy workout for Saturday (2 to 3 hours), and save a long, hard workout for Sunday (1½ to 2½ hours). Monday is for resting. Climbing or skiing over the weekend counts toward the long workout—that's what I'm training for. Monday's rest is certainly crucial for healing overexerted muscles, but I find it even more important for keeping up my interest. Take a day off and you'll be more excited about getting rolling the next day.

It is important to monitor your body during each workout; otherwise you might push harder than you should for a slow recovery workout and compromise a hard one; or you might coast through a hard workout and not gain the maximum benefit from it. By checking your pulse rate you can accurately monitor each day's training. Your pulse is the tachometer of a workout. It indicates how hard you are pushing your body.

To determine your pulse rate during a workout, stop and count your heartbeats for 15 seconds, and then multiply that number by four. If you don't want to stop, you can use a heart-rate monitor. I use one with a wireless sending unit that straps around the chest and a wristwatch that displays my pulse rate. The figure you get from your calculations or a monitor should fall within your **training range.** If your pulse is too low, you should speed up. If it's too high, ease off a bit.

To estimate your training range, first determine your maximum pulse rate by subtracting your age from 225. Your training range should fall between 70 percent and 80 percent of the maximum rate. If you are thirty-two, for example, your maximum pulse rate is 193 beats per minute and should range between 135 and 154 during training. Note that this is a rough guideline that varies according to your fitness and the altitude.

On easy days, stay near the lower end of your training range, around 70 percent of your maximum. (See Note below.) Concentrate on keeping your pulse down because you want your body to rest for the harder workouts. On hard days get closer to the 80 percent mark, which will mean that your body is approaching its **anaerobic threshold:** the stage at which you get "pumped." These hard days require the most recovery time.

Once you have a good aerobic base, you can increase your speed through specific training: alternately crossing and retreating from your anaerobic threshold. With this kind of training your body will grow accustomed to a higher energy output and greater speed. A spontaneous sort of speed training that I enjoy is called *fartlek,* a Swedish term for speed play. During *fartlek* you increase your speed at random and slow the pace for recovery when you tire. For instance, when on my bicycle on a course with rolling hills I jam on the ups and rest on the downs. Cross-country ski courses tend to force these kinds of demands on the skier: shorter, intense pushes uphill with fast glides down.

A more regimented kind of speed training is **intervals.** When doing intervals you closely monitor alternating periods of high-energy output and recovery. With anaerobic intervals you extend yourself past your 80 percent mark for a short time (usually between 30 seconds and 3 minutes), then slow for recovery until your pulse drops to 100 beats. Time the recovery period. When it takes markedly longer than the first interval for your pulse to drop, you have done enough intervals.

For intervals—and any kind of speed training—it is important to be well rested and have a good training base. Warm up, stretch, and warm down. Start off with very short intervals, and don't push too hard. Too little speed training won't do you any harm—it is too *much* speed training that injures many athletes. Consult a good running, cycling, or ski-racing book to set up a speed-training schedule.

Note: The above percentages represent a general, more traditional approach to training. The percentages of how much you exercise at what level do vary. Today some experts indicate that too much of this "middle" output—70 percent maximum heart rate (MHR)—and not enough very slow distance, balanced with high-output workouts, just gets you stuck in that middle in a long, slow rut. In Rob Sleamaker's book *Serious Training for*

Serious Athletes, he suggests—even for casual athletes—slower slow days and more frequent, faster fast days. In other words, more work on either end of your range. This approach has proven very effective and time-efficient for many athletes. For the specifics, I recommend consulting his book, and experimenting with what works for you.

CROSS-COUNTRY AND IN-LINE SKATING

The evolution of classic cross-country technique to skating has done more to improve my downhill skiing than any other activity. The movements for snow skating are easy to duplicate on pavement. It's not only fun but it's muscle-specific for downhill as well as cross-country ski training. Skates with in-line wheels or roller skis designed for skating are your best choice for skate training. Add long cross-country skating poles and you will effectively train your upper as well as your lower body. There are several good books on skating available. Find one you like. Find a smooth pavement, too—you will feel every bump on those tiny wheels.

STRENGTH TRAINING

Those of us who enjoy aerobic sports are often on the scrawny side, but as skiers we need strength for leg-pumping crud, packing a big load into a backcountry cabin, or squeezing off that last desperate turn. Most important, specific-strength training makes a skier more resistant to injury. Pushups, situps (the abdomen is especially important to skiers), pullups, squats, leg curls, and all sorts of calisthenics are simple, effective strength builders. Today's gyms usually have a personal trainer who can set you up with a good program and, most importantly, with the right technique.

It usually takes some kind of toy or apparatus to keep me interested in strength-training my legs. Nautilus® is a great workout, but it isn't always available and is not very portable. For maximum portability there are several stretch devices for strength and flexibility training. These are tools that, when attached to a fixed object, can be pulled in different directions to exercise specific muscles.

My favorite of these is the sport cord (rubber tubing, sometimes with handles). It was introduced to me by U.S. Ski Team Trainer John Atkins as part of my recuperative program after knee surgery. A very simple, portable training device, the sport cord was developed for athletes' specific-strength training and is used both as a preventative against injury and as part of a recuperative program after injury. It provides a great workout.

Regardless of your choice of exercise, keeping yourself excited about being fit is the key to success. Choose training activities that are fun, like skating and cycling, and that exercise the right muscle groups for skiing. Rest to preserve your enthusiasm for each session, and alternate the difficulty of various sessions. You will find yourself fitter, and your skiing more fun and enjoyable.

Photo on following pages
© Mark Shapiro

© Paul Parker

ADVANCED
SKILLS

Skating

Learn to skate on your tele skis. I use the skate everywhere: traversing cat roads, accelerating on flat downhills, getting from one lift to another. In the backcountry, an efficient skate on your tele or randonnée boards can quickly get you past what would be interminable flats, plodding with skins on your skis.

If you want to get into skating for its own sake, try cross-country ski skating. There are good books available on the different techniques. For now I'll outline simple skating on heavy, metal-edged boards.

SKATING EXERCISES

Start by practicing the herringbone (see the chapter Basic Parallel Turns). Once that feels comfortable, change terrain to a very gradual uphill. This will allow you to get a bit of glide. Now, as you step from one ski to the other, give a little push to glide on the new ski. You should be using the same duck-footed position as with the herringbone, but push a little harder from one ski to the other, and let each ski glide before the next push.

Now try the next step: as you push off of one ski onto the other (gliding) ski, try to put the gliding ski down on its outside edge. That's right, its *outside* edge. Transfer your weight completely to that gliding ski—no hanging back on the pushing one.

OK, now the flats. Pick a flat, hard-packed area. On the hill, it was probably hard to actually put your gliding ski down on its outside edge, but thinking about the outside edge got your ski flat so that it would glide. In the flats, you can really do it. See how in illustration 33 the skier comes down on that ski on its outside edge? The weight shifts from the pushing ski to the outside edge of the gliding ski. Then that gliding ski is rolled over onto its inside edge for the next push.

Photo on preceding page
© John Norris

33
Skating on tele skis

If you feel like you're "stuck" between your feet, try making more of a V with your skis and push from one side of the V to the other. Let your body sway from side to side, from your pushing edge to your gliding edge, and completely commit your weight to that outside gliding edge. Drive your hips directly over the new gliding ski with each skate.

As you get your weight shift down, you can push off on your poles at the same time. Downhill-length poles aren't the best for skating—they're too short for much power—but they will add a bit of balance and rhythm to your skating. Pushing on your poles with each skating motion on each side is what cross-country skiers call V2.

Here's another exercise. Focusing on the inside and outside corners of your boots, try skating from the inside corner of the boot on your pushing ski to the outside corner of the boot on your gliding ski. For some skiers, especially those with stiff boots, it's easier to use this inside corner, outside corner approach (see "The Inside Corner" in the chapter Advanced Parallel Tips).

KEY SKATING POINTS

Skating is a natural movement that most of us have practiced during our first or subsequent childhoods on roller skates, in-line skates, ice skates, alpine skis, or skating skis. Skating on these tele boards is no different. The key points are as follows:

- Make a shallow V with your skis—be sure that they aren't parallel.
- Make a complete weight shift from pushing to gliding ski.
- Put the gliding ski down on (or almost on) its outside edge.
- Feel the pressure on the inside corner of your pushing boot, and the outside corner of your gliding boot.

Perfect your skating and you'll learn to control your edges. As your gliding ski becomes your new pushing ski, you'll feel yourself roll from its outside gliding edge to its inside pushing one. You'll feel the total commitment from pushing edge to gliding edge. This is a key in advanced skiing and a major emphasis in this book: learning to control not only the outside ski in a turn, but the inside ski and its uphill edge as well. Controlling that uphill, or inside, ski and its edge opens the door to expert teles and parallel turns.

Advanced Telemark Tips

In the early telemark days, the back ski acted as a rudder while the front ski did most of the work. A flatter, less-weighted back ski created elegant, long-radius arcs in soft snow but was a disaster on harder snow. That is probably one reason why the telemark had a short first life. As soon as Rudolph Lettner, an Austrian metalworker, put metal edges on a pair of skis and skiers like Hannes Schneider got hold of a pair, telemark was put out to pasture and skiers were ripping, arcing the Arlberg.

In these modern days of telemark, skiers are determined to ski all conditions using the genuflecting turn, so technique has had to evolve. So has equipment: plastic boots and sophisticated alpine-like skis flexed for the telemark turn facilitate arcs that rival any alpine turn—if you don't neglect that back ski.

TUCKING YOUR BACK LEG

When I think of a series of good tele turns, I think of a horse. I liked horses before I discovered skis. When I really wanted to get my horse—his name was John—to perform, I would first get him collected. I would rein him in, signaling him to prepare for anything: a quick turn, a jump, a skid-stop. John knew the signal. He would collect his big body into a "ready" posture rather than trotting along, spread out. He would perk up as though he had just seen a snake and was preparing to bolt.

In your telemark, try "collecting" yourself by tucking your rear leg under you and bringing your body into its most athletic position. Don't leave your back leg flapping in the breeze like a wounded dog (a "doggie leg"); keep it under you where you can use it (see illus. 34). Like John's, your body should feel collected and ready to bolt. It's that athletic position that we discussed earlier in the book: stomach in, lower back relaxed.

Photo on preceding page
© Scott Cramer

34
Tuck your rear leg

Try pinching your buttocks together as though you are holding a C-note between your cheeks. This helps tuck that leg and tighten your stance fore-to-aft. You'll feel aggressive, ready for anything.

POINTING YOUR KNEE

Telemark or parallel, I do a lot of pointing with my knees. You'll pick up these "pointy-knee" ideas throughout this book. Some coaches call them "sharp knees."

Start your turns thinking of your front knee as a headlight. With each turn, sweep the headlight beam toward your new destination. This focus will enhance the edging and steering of your front ski.

Now try thinking of your back knee as the headlight. Forget your front one for a minute; point your back (inside) knee into the new turn. Once the front knee/headlight becomes automatic, I prefer to focus on this back knee (see illus. 35).

35
Point your front and your back knees into the turn

USING YOUR BIG TOE, LITTLE TOE

This is something that sticks in many of my students' minds: "big toe, little toe." The big-toe, little-toe idea is simple: when you edge your skis into a turn, you should feel the pressure under the big-toe side (inside-edge side) of your front foot and the little-toe side (outside-edge side) of your rear foot. This will edge your skis properly. Notice that it's not just the big toe and little toe that get the focus: it's that whole side of each foot that edges the ski.

For most skiers it's the little-toe part of this idea that really gets results. Thinking about the weight under the little-toe side of that back foot edges your back (uphill) ski (see illus. 36). Edging and weighting your back ski is the key to preventing those "spinning out" turns.

Be aware of your foot position on your rear ski; avoid "tiptoeing" on it, hinging your boots up on their toes. Keep your entire forefoot on the ski.

If you feel the rear ski sliding out from under you, concentrate more pressure on the *little-toe side* of the rear foot. If you have trouble initiating your turns (a less frequent problem), concentrate more pressure on the big-toe side of the front foot.

DROPPING YOUR REAR HEEL

In the Basic Telemark chapter you learned to emphasize the weight on your inside (rear) ski. Now I've added "big toe, little toe," the little-toe idea further emphasizing *edging* the rear ski. *Weighting and edging* the rear ski in your telemark will give you better control of your turn.

Your rear ski should bear at least half of your body weight—it seems like even more in certain kinds of snow. You can tell that you have enough weight back there when you feel the Achilles tendon and calf of your rear leg stretch. You will automatically tuck your hips under you to ease that tension.

For your next telemark turn go one step further. *Relax and bend your rear ankle* so your heel drops closer to the ski. Stay on edge, of course; but try to get as much of your rear foot onto the ski as possible (see illustrations 35 and 36). The more foot you have on that back ski the more weight it gets, and the better you will be able to control it through the finish of each turn.

DOING MORE WITH YOUR HIPS

An expert tele skier will look very similar to an alpine skier—from the waist up. The quiet upper body is always facing down the hill. But the radical differences between the leads of the two turns result in two very different postures from the waist down.

In illustration 37 notice how the tele skier's hips punch through the turn, setting the skis on their edges and using the big hip muscles to keep them there. His upper body acts as though it's separated from his lower body, facing quietly downhill as the skis arc back and forth. As I punch this hip around, I feel the pressure under the arch of my front foot.

When you use your hips to turn you must concentrate even more on facing your torso down the hill. When you make a turn, the downhill hip rotates and your torso twists the other way. With skis and hips turning, and chest and navel always facing the fall line, your body acts as a coiled spring ready to be released. When you release your edges, those stretched back muscles and contracted stomach muscles whip your skis into the next arc. Your turns snap around effortlessly from all of that stored energy.

37
Tele-anticipation: chest facing down the hill, hips cranking the turn

This is **tele-anticipation**—upper body and hands always facing down the hill in anticipation of the new turn. In this position I feel my abdomen getting a workout: the downhill (outside) muscles of my abdomen contracted, the uphill muscles of my abdomen (and lower back) stretched.

Use your abdomen as much as you can. The more you anticipate, especially with the tele's advanced outside hip, the more your abdomen will work for you. If you feel your abdominal muscles in each turn, then you are probably doing it right.

TIMING YOUR EDGING

If you initiate your teles by stemming a front ski and *then* transferring weight to the rear ski, you're doing a two-step kind of turn. Technicians call this a **sequential turn initiation** because the skis are edged in a one-two sequence. This "step-telemark" is covered later in this book. It is one of those sequential turns used for moguls and hairy terrain. Its quick directional change allows you to "walk" down otherwise formidable slopes. I do not recommend it as your standard turn.

I prefer to edge my skis *at the same time* in a **simultaneous turn initiation**. It's a bit more difficult but much more fluid and effective in working the skis. It carves them, as opposed to turning them with one-two moves that use stepping, steering, and skidding.

Try this more fluid series of movements the next time you link teles. As you rise between turns, keep both skis flat—in "neutral"—during your lead change. Once the correct foot is forward for the new turn, put it in gear and *edge both skis at the same time* for the next turn. Tip the skis over, pressuring them under the big-toe side of your front foot and the little-toe side of your rear foot—at exactly the same time.

Simultaneous edging is a very smooth style of skiing (see illus. 38). With it, you can often eliminate stepping to feel your way into questionable snow conditions. You'll more confidently arc through difficult snow.

The next step in timing your edging focuses on the start of the turn. When initiating the turn, try to initiate it with the *uphill edge of your back ski*—your "little-toe" ski. Do this by trying to make that back-ski edge the first thing that contacts the snow when you change leads.

Just now, I said edge at the same time; now I'm trying to get on that edge even sooner. It helps some advanced skiers to think of this as *dropping their rear leg back* into a tele as they start the turn rather than moving the front leg forward. This way, that rear leg already has the focus.

Don't worry about the front ski for now; for most advanced telemark

38
Edge both skis at
the same time

skiers the front ski's edging and steering is an automatic movement in their lead change. Focus on edging and weighting that back ski. You don't need to lean back—keep your body position normal. Just drop that foot back into a tele, and get on that edge earlier.

Why? With this exercise you can avoid sequential movements to initiate the turn: that "one-two" stepping movement that some skiers use when they edge the front ski first, then edge and finish the arc on the back ski. That takes more time. I'd rather get both skis arced and turning together. Focusing on edging your back ski first really gets both skis edging and turning at the same time. I've found that when I use this focus on hard snow or in grabby, tricky snow, my skis will pick the same arc rather than converging or diverging as they so often do in crud—especially using one-two moves.

Try it. Go out and make some arcs focusing on turn initiation with that back-ski edge.

Now try steering that back ski. Steer it—twist it—with your forefoot into the new turn as you edge it. It's a different feel from steering a ski with your heel down, as in a wedge turn; you direct the ski with your forefoot. Edge it and steer it with your forefoot at the initiation of your turn.

As you add this back-ski emphasis, especially once you steer your back ski, you'll find your skis drifting apart a little, widening your stance. You might even feel that the front and back skis are diverging a bit, rather than the common converging (wedging) that characterizes most skiers' telemarks. That's good. A wider stance will help you edge and steer your skis equally into each new turn. Through the turn, keep weighting, steering, and edging that back ski, and your skis will stay wider, more parallel. This wider, parallel-ski tele stance is more effective not only in soft and difficult snow, but also on hard snow, allowing you to better edge the back ski with a more stable side-to-side platform.

It's unlikely, but if you find yourself doing a "wheelie" with an ineffectual front ski, make a few of your normal turns to get back into a rhythm, then focus on the back-ski edge. Feel how much more you can use the back ski, rather than trailing it behind into the finish of the turn. In advanced skiing, your back ski—or inside ski in parallel—is an important tool to build the right angles between the snow, your edges, and the rest of your body.

BACK SKI REVIEW

In alpine turns you vary your weight distribution between skis according to the snow conditions. Often—especially on hard snow—you're skiing with your weight on one ski at a time. Telemark, however, is almost always a two-ski turn. I've given the back ski a lot of emphasis in this assortment of ski tips not because it's more important than the front ski, but because it's the most often neglected.

Below is a summary of the pointers that I've given above. These exercises will help you weight, control, and arc your back ski. There are a lot of different tips listed. In an on-snow class, it would take at least a couple of days to present all of them—and much longer for the students to practice and absorb them. Be patient; take your time. It's important to think about these things *one at a time.* They are all exercises to achieve the same end—controlling and using the rear ski—so choose the one that works best for you. Refer to the illustrations in this chapter for a good image.

- Tuck your leg. If you feel as if your telemark stance is too long and spread out, you may not be able to properly weight the back ski. Notice how in illustration 34 the skier's rear leg is tucked under the body so that it can be weighted, not so far back that he's up on his tiptoes. Think of pointing that back knee straight down at the ski; or, pinch your buttocks together and your legs will naturally come together into a more "collected" stance.
- Point your front knee like a headlight, shining it into each new turn.
- Point your back knee like a headlight, shining it into each new turn (illus. 35).
- Think "big toe, little toe." Feel pressure on your edges under the big-toe side of your front foot, and the little-toe side of your back foot (illus. 36).
- Drop your heel. Think of dropping your back heel closer to the ski, pressing on the ball of your back foot (little-toe side) instead of cranking up on your toes. Keep as much of that back foot on the ski as you can (illus. 35).
- Relax and bend the ankle of your back leg through the turn. Flex it as much as you can. This will drop your heel and allow you to get more pressure on the ball of that rear foot.
- Try edging both skis at the same time, emphasizing the uphill edge of the back ski (illus. 38).
- When initiating a turn, slide your rear foot back rather than your front foot forward. This will keep you centered between your skis rather than too far forward, and will keep your rear ski doing much more of the work. It also helps on very steep slopes, reducing that feeling of "diving" down the hill and accelerating uncontrollably.
- Once you are very comfortable with edging both skis at the same time, try initiating your turns with the inside edge of your back ski. Your front ski's steering and edging should be a reflex action by now; think about your rear ski and starting your turns with the inside edge of that ski. Are you using both skis? Get the most from them; get your money's worth. There's no sense in just using half a pair. Pressure, weight, and arc that back ski for rounder, more controlled turns. You won't believe the difference.

▲ © John Norris

Photos on
preceding pages
© John Norris

◀ © Scott Cramer

▲ © John Norris

▼ © Paul Parker

▶ © Ace Kvale

▲ © Mark Shapiro

▲ © Paul Parker

▶ © Mark Shapiro

▲ © John Norris

▼ © Ace Kvale

▲ © John Norris

Skiing the Silvretta's Jamtal

~

The wind whistled all night. Morning dawned as one of those weird, hazy days in the Alps that signals a big change. On days like that it either clears or it hits the fan, but it doesn't stay the same. We got an early start, crunching over the bulletproof crust. Our group moved fast; we had a long day ahead and didn't want to get stuck in the fog on a featureless glacier. It had snowed just enough to drift into dense, impenetrable booby traps that could disappear in flat light.

We climbed the pass from the Swiss Tuoi hut toward the Austrian Jamtal hut. Climbing was a little scary, the wind's loading having left perfect man-traps that could break loose and carry a skier rapidly over the steep, hard crust underneath. Starting a little avalanche wouldn't be such a big deal, but on that exposed climb an unarrested slide could be serious.

On top of the *Jamjoch* (pass) the Jamtal *Ferner* (glacier) began, stretching down to the Jamtal hut. It was a long, medium-angle slope, not many crevasses, perfect on a powder day, questionable after last night's wind. Our descent was on the lee side of the pass, on the Swiss-Austrian border.

We peeled off our skins, surveying our descent. The glacier was covered with powder artfully sculpted into *sastrugi* ridges. It looked difficult, so we mulled over technique tricks for staying upright. It was a custom among our group—old ski buddies—to discuss which was the key turn or move from our bag of survival-skiing tricks. Sort of like which wine would be the best with dinner.

Ankles. That was the key.

We've always been told to bend our knees. Knees allow the legs to function as pistons and shock absorbers, extending to pressure and arc the ski, flexing to lighten and absorb that pressure. Yet for me, it's thinking about my ankles that bends my knees. Parallel or telemark, with relaxed ankles that are extended and flexed through the turn, my knees bend naturally and my body stays centered over the skis.

Evaluating the smooth, windblown, trackless snow below, we agreed that ankles it was. Before talking further, I checked out the snow, making a few "demo" turns, exaggerating the flexing and extending of my ankles. It worked; my skis scribed round, controlled turns through the stiff, wind-blown powder.

Mountains in Europe are big, with lots of vertical. Below us was the Jamtal Ferner's 3000-foot glacier descent—plenty of room for practice. After too much discussion, each of us got our cranky old ankles moving. The snow was interesting—and skiable. Ankles got us arcing turns until, breathless, we had to stop. We kept telling ourselves as our legs got pumped that we needed to use the full range of motion in our ankles to extend and absorb through the turns. For the last fifty turns we could smell the hot soup; we were ready for a break before the long slog up the last pass. The sun was dropping behind the ridge for that last descent—the last move we'd need would be for breakable crust.

© Paul Parker

Advanced Parallel Tips

Parallel turns are much more effective than telemarks on hard snow or in narrow and precipitous terrain. When you must face the fall line on a steep slope, the parallel turn's stance is stronger and more stable than the rotated position of the telemark. So even if it's not telemarker's dogma, to be as versatile as possible you can and should perfect your parallel turns.

Work on your basic parallel and accumulate some mileage. Make enough parallel turns so that you can use them on any moderate terrain. Practice your stem christies, which are useful when you need a very quick turn initiation. Once you've logged those miles, the next step is to develop your all-terrain parallel. You will want to make parallel turns in difficult conditions. You will want to make them instinctively.

To hone your turns we'll work on these things: flexing your ankles, timing your edge change, directing your uphill knee, and feeling your edge under a certain part of your foot. As we did in the tele section, we'll switch the focus from the outside ski to the inside ski. These are all tricks that will transform your basic parallel turns into dependable, all-terrain maneuvers.

USING YOUR ANKLES

Alpine instructors always tell students to bend their knees. Knees, when flexed, act as shock absorbers. Bending them lowers your center of balance and increases your stability. Without knee-bend you couldn't flex and extend your legs to weight and unweight your skis and control your edge pressure. Articulating your knees also facilitates angulation, both at the knee joints and at the hips.

Bend your knees, everyone.

But that's not the whole point of my focus. You must also *bend your ankles*. If you bend your knees and not your ankles you'll fall on your butt. More realistically, without flexible ankles your "shock absorbers" disappear. Your

Photo on preceding page
© Scott Cramer

skis skid. With every little variation in the snow your weight goes to the extremes, either too far forward or too far back. You try to compensate, and your body bends at the waist—that's the "feeding-chicken" stance.

Ankle bend is an especially important focus for anyone with plastic boot cuffs—alpine or tele—because the cuffs' stiffness takes a more concerted effort to flex. It's easy to spot skiers whose boots are too stiff. They are broken at the waist, clucking down the hill.

Let's ski and think about ankles. Relax in your athletic, rounded ski stance: stomach in, back relaxed. Push off down the slope and gain some momentum. Start with medium-radius, "skiddy" parallel turns, concentrating on smoothly extending and flexing your ankles as you extend and sink through each arc. Extend your legs at the beginning of the turn by extending both of your ankles. Doing this I feel centered, pushing down on my toes as I make this extension. At the high point of your "standing up," your extension, begin to sink through the rest of the turn, again at the ankles (see illus. 39). Finish with ankles totally flexed. Again you'll be centered; avoid finishing the turns on your toes or heels.

Keep making these skiddy parallels, exaggerating the ankle movement. In stiffer boots it helps to think about *pulling up on your toes* to get a good bend in your ankles as you sink through the turn.

You're on a packed slope, so your weight emphasis should be on your outside foot. Try to feel your weight on your whole outside foot—not just on your toes or heel.

MAKING SMOOTHER TURNS

Basic parallel turns are very abrupt and use lots of hard steering movements. Everything happens at once. But in all but the smoothest groomed snow conditions, free-heel skiers can't afford these edge-catching, exaggerated movements. Free-heel parallels have to be smooth and extra-efficient.

You can pull off a smooth and elegant parallel turn by shifting your weight to the uphill ski earlier, *before* starting the next turn. Try it. Begin with a traverse, pushing off to gain a little speed. Now stand up tall and shift your weight to the *uphill edge of your uphill ski*. Once you have shifted weight to that uphill edge, *then*—no earlier!—tip the ski over into a turn, rolling it onto its inside edge for your next turn. Voila! It becomes your outside ski. Feel how your body seeks the fall line as you smoothly change edges and steer both skis into the turn? Don't resist; let your body succumb to gravity, down the fall line.

39
Extend and flex
your ankles

Try it again. Sink through your last turn. As your skis come across the hill and your body finishes its sinking motion, immediately start the rise back up. Stand up tall; when your lower leg is extended, continue your upward movement by shifting to the *uphill edge of your uphill ski*. Once you're shifted to that uphill ski's edge, then move into the next turn. Focus your eyes down the hill and let your body move ahead of your skis, in the new direction (see illus. 40).

If you can think of moving your body into the new turn, your skis will tip over automatically. If it's too abstract for you to think of what your body is doing, think of *tipping* the uphill ski over into the new turn, or rolling it onto its inside edge. Either way you want to think about it, the move into the new turn starts *after* you've shifted your weight to the uphill edge of the uphill ski. Practice on a roomy slope; be patient; and don't start that new turn until your weight is shifted.

40
Shift your weight to your
uphill ski before starting
the next turn

FOCUSING ON THE INSIDE SKI

In the telemark section I really emphasized the back foot, the inside foot. That is an obvious focus for tele skiers; when you don't use that foot, you spin out.

The inside ski is no less necessary for parallel skiing. We neglect that ski in parallel instruction because the first big hurdle is getting skiers to shift their weight confidently to the outside ski. Once you get over that hurdle and develop a weight shift, it doesn't mean that you can ski only on your weighted outside ski and forget the inside one. On the contrary, the inside ski is an important key to the most advanced turns. Although many of the exercises and drills that instructors use focus on the outside foot, you must use your inside ski. An inside ski focus—knowing what to do with it—will transform your turns from tentative tacks to confident arcs.

In the following section of tips, I want you to forget your outside ski for awhile. As we did in the advanced telemark turns, let's assume (can we?) that you've practiced enough so that your outside ski is getting the weight and edging that it needs, with movements almost automatic. We'll shift our emphasis to the inside ski to develop your bombproof parallel.

Focus on Your Inside Knee

Have you crossed your tips making parallel turns? It's hard to get a good edge set on the topsheet of your bottom ski. It happens to the best skiers; often they accidentally cross their tips because they're overemphasizing the outside foot and forgetting the inside one, enthusiastically skiing the outside ski right over the top of it. In a steep couloir, that's a bummer.

Your inside ski must be *steered* (twisted to point it in the desired direction) and *edged* (tipped onto its edge) just like the outside ski. By focusing on your inside knee, you set up your body for quicker, easier moves.

Think of leading each new turn with your *inside knee*. Each time you initiate a new turn, focus on pointing the new inside knee in the direction of that turn (some call that the uphill knee or ski). It might feel as though you are taking a hard corner on a bicycle, leaning into the turn with your inside knee. Emphasizing the inside knee, you'll also point the inside ski's tip in the direction of the new turn (see illus. 41).

This simple steering move with your inside knee, foot, and ski will make your turns much quicker and easier and will eliminate a stemming motion that can result in crossed tips in difficult snow and slides for life on steep terrain. On the steeps, think of "leading," or starting, the turn with that knee.

41
Point your inside knee
(toe and ski tip) into
the new turn

That gets your body aligned for the turn and moves your inside ski out of the way early, so that the outside ski can do its stuff without crossing over it.

Edge Your Inside Ski

Skis that are edged equally are more likely to stay parallel. When you step onto one ski at a time in loose snow, your skis tend to wander off in different directions—especially with free heels. On hard snow, unequally edged skis often cross. To avoid the splits or cross-tipped slammers, you must tip both skis over onto their edges at the same time (see illus. 41).

Try it: make a series of turns and consciously focus on edging your inside ski. The inside ski doesn't need much weight for this edge to make a difference. Get used to the idea of edging the skis at the same time. Don't edge one and then the other. Tip your skis onto their new inside edges simultaneously.

Note: in deep snow, edging doesn't mean that the edge is gripping into firm snow; it means that the ski is tipped over onto its edge. It's still the same movement.

Think "Light as a Feather"

Skiers often ask how much weight they should put on their inside ski during parallel turns. On groomed and firm snow that ski is much lighter than the outside one. This doesn't mean that it's less important; so it's best to work with the last two exercises first before thinking much about weight. Those ideas get us steering and edging the inside ski.

OK, for this exercise on packed, refrozen, or windblown snow, make parallel turns, thinking "light as a feather" on your inside ski. As you shift your weight to your new outside ski, think light on the new inside one. This focus is especially useful in hard conditions when you need a good edge. *Light as a feather.*

Slide the Inside Ski Forward

Sliding this inside foot forward as you finish your turn allows you to get a better edge with both skis. It faces your torso and pelvis into the fall line. Try it. As your skis come out of the fall line, let that inside ski slide forward before you shift your weight to it and start a new turn (again, see illus. 41). Think back to the earlier exercise, "Making Smoother Turns." Let that inside ski slide forward as you round your last turn, so that it's ahead when you make that early weight shift.

Weight the Inside Ski

We've been working on "light as a feather" on the inside foot. But in different conditions, you will learn to vary this weight distribution. Using a deep-snow parallel, you must put weight on the inside ski so that it doesn't wander with a mind of its own. It's easiest for me to think about my feet: as my skis come into the fall line in deep snow, I flex my ankles and *pressure that inside foot on its whole little-toe side.* Try it. Put enough weight on that inside foot to feel pressure on its little-toe side.

Use your inside foot and play with your weight distribution. In light, loose snow you will ski with almost equal weight distribution between your feet. In heavier loose snow, you may put a little more weight on the outside ski. On hard snow, you may have almost all your weight on the outside ski. This difference will depend on the heaviness of the snow, the base underneath, and the stiffness of your skis. The goal is the same: to get both skis to arc and float equally. This is done through steering, edging, and weighting (or lightening) the inside ski.

KNEE-TO-BOOT CHASERS

"Knee-to-boot chasers" help you get your skis out to the side, away from your body, and up on their edges for more carving and less skidding. Knee-to-boot chasers will help you make a more technical turn. Skiing with your feet in a hip-width stance, "chase" your inside (uphill) boot with your outside (downhill) knee. *Tip that inside boot away* so that the knee can't catch it. Notice how your skis are tipped up on their edges (see illus. 42).

42
"Knee-to-boot chasers"

THE INSIDE CORNER

Next try a similar idea with a different focus: move into the "inside corner" of your boot. As shown in illustration 43, put your hands on the fronts of your boot cuffs. Now think of your boots as though they have four corners.

43
Hands on the fronts
of your boot cuffs

Move your hands to the inside (or uphill) corner of each boot, as shown in illustration 44. Press your shins toward your hands and toward the uphill corners. This inside corner is where you should press your shins as you move into each new turn.

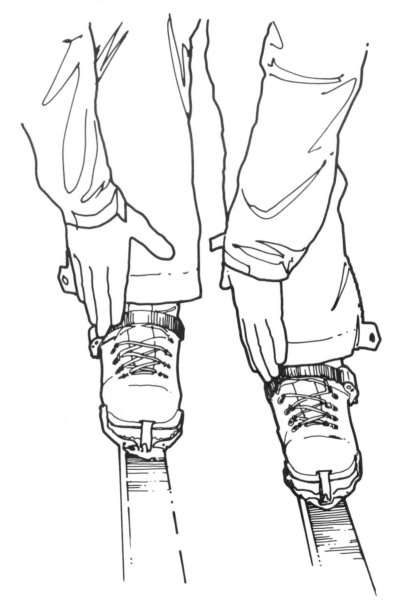

44
Hands on the "inside corners"; press your shins toward these corners as you move into a turn

36
Edge on the big-toe side
of your front foot and
the little-toe side of
your back foot

In alpine skiing the pelvis faces more directly down the hill—the hips
are "open" to the hill—with the uphill ski ahead of the downhill one. A
tele skier, however, has the downhill ski advanced, so the hips rotate with
the turn rather than facing downhill. I think of it as *punching* my downhill
hip around.

Now make a series of turns, consciously initiating each by pressing into both inside corners—don't press straight forward. Stick with the corners all the way through the turn. Your body should move gracefully into the fall line, the skis well-edged throughout the arc.

DRIVING YOUR HEELS

Try a completely different focus: your heels. This is an idea that will get more rebound and snap from advanced turns. Since your heels aren't fastened down, it also helps keep your balance centered in a stable position to reduce the chance of a forward fall.

Carve a few smooth arcs, feeling the weight on your whole outside foot throughout the turn. Now change your focus and think about the heel of your foot. As you round the bend and your skis come out of the fall line, drive your heels toward the finish of the arc. That's right. Try to push your heels ahead. Don't sit back. Just think heels, weighting your feet from the arch backward.

These movements don't merely emphasize your feet and legs. By focusing on specific lower-body movements and sensations, your upper body wants to move in the right direction—in the direction of the next turn. You'll soon find yourself seeking the fall line with your torso and skiing more aggressively in the manner described in the chapter Skiing from the Waist Up. Your turns will become indistinguishable from those of a strong alpine skier.

Photo on following pages
© Mark Shapiro

REFINEMENT

More Free-heel Turns

Motion is what makes your skis go round. Flexion and extension lighten and pressure your skis at the proper moment in each arc to get the most from your skis for as little effort as possible.

The low, bent-kneed position of the classic telemark has influenced many free-heel skiers to stay locked in a genuflecting position throughout their tele turns—or stuck in a crouch in parallel turns. *Locked* is the word; there is little maneuverability once down there, and crouching low often results in a pair of sore knees. Bruised and broken patellae are common among low-flying telemarkers whose rear knees skim the snow. Trolling with your kneecaps is a good way to find stumps and rocks.

If you learn to contract and extend your legs, what was once a static, too-low position gives way to a fluid flexion and extension movement. In parallel or telemark turning you need this flexion and extension to control the pressure that builds as your skis come across the fall line. Your skis are most likely to skid at the finish of each turn as they come across the hill. Once across the fall line they resist the force of gravity that is pulling your body downhill and increasing the pressure against your edges. If you do not lighten your skis to absorb this excess pressure they will begin to "chatter."

On hard snow we instinctively want to stiffen and straighten our legs to resist chatter, but the best thing to do is to lighten the skis by flexing at the ankles, sinking and absorbing that pressure on the edges. In order to have the necessary range of motion to make this flexing movement, you should be tall early in the turn—otherwise you will have nowhere to sink.

Photo on preceding page
© Mark Shapiro

THE "NOW" TURN

There is a great skiing exercise called the **now** turn (some call it the **patience** turn) to emphasize this feeling of motion. I have used it successfully with many free-heel students with unanimous results. These students improved their turning rhythm, their maneuverability, and their pressure control on their edges. The now turn emphasizes a tall, extended position by delaying the sinking motion until the skis are directly in the fall line.

Find a wide, moderate slope. Using either parallel or telemark turning technique, stand very tall. Stay in this tall position until you reach *now*. *Now* is when your skis are in the fall line. *Be patient; don't sink until your skis are pointing directly down the hill.* Say "now" out loud, and sink into the turn finish once your skis are in the fall line. When sinking, be sure that you flex at the *ankles and knees*, not at the waist.

Link a sequence of now turns down the hill, concentrating on first standing tall, then delaying the sinking motion. The turns won't be round; they will have a sort of J shape (see illus. 45). You will notice that the extension-flexion of your legs creates more rhythm in your skiing. Feel how smoothly and crisply your skis finish each turn as the sinking lightens the pressure on your edges and tightens your turn finish. At first the up-and-down motion might feel exaggerated, but you'll soon find that it makes your skis snap around more smoothly and quickly.

Whether you parallel or telemark, the elements are the same. Don't throw out your low position. Ski *through* it with dynamic, rhythmic flexion and extension motions.

THE TELEMARK TWO-STEP

I'm not wild about "steppy," sequential turns unless you really need them. However, the step-telemark is an important technique to have in your quiver, especially for controlled, steered turns on radically steep and bumpy terrain. In grabby crud you can step the front ski across the hill to "feel" the snow, then check your speed with the rear one.

In certain situations it isn't necessarily a regression to choose sequential step-turning techniques rather than simultaneous ones. Sometimes you have to skid your skis in order to turn more quickly. These are spots where, if you spend too much time carving through the fall line, you will pick up uncontrollable speed.

Step-telemarks are a quicker, more advanced version of the half-wedge telemark. Pick a gentle, packed slope and push off into the fall line. Move from a straight parallel run into a telemark by stepping your front ski into a stem. That's right. Step the front ski not only into the lead but with the ski stemmed, steering it into a new turn.

When stepping the front ski in a stem across the hill, you will be into your turn quickly. Brace your weight against the edge of the front ski and

45
"Now" turns

quickly step the rear ski alongside it, edging the snow hard with the uphill edge of your rear ski. "Sting" the snow with the rear ski as you put it down. I like to count to myself: "one (front step), two (rear step)," and so on (see illus. 46).

46
Step-telemarks; think
"one, two, one, two, . . . "

Now add a pole plant, *stinging the snow with your downhill pole* as you sting the snow with the edge of the rear ski. I think: "one, sting, one, sting; one (front step), sting (rear step and pole plant), one, sting, one, sting." Practice it on the flats at slow speeds. It feels as though you are "walking" down the hill, checking your speed with each ski/edge sting. With a little practice you can walk down anything—steeps, bumps, catchy crud. Remember, the rear ski controls your speed, so edge it fast and hard with your little toe when you step it around.

It's not the most elegant technique, but the step-telemark is a godsend for controlling your speed in hairy situations. The more tools like jump turns and step-teles that you learn, the more fun you'll have when the skiing's not perfect.

© John Norris

A HYBRID TURN

Telemarks are indispensable in cruddy snow, very deep powder, crust, or any condition that yanks your feet back as momentum drags your body forward. But parallel turns are often more secure on hard and refrozen snow, when falling forward is less likely but side-to-side stability is elusive. There's a hybrid turn that combines the advantages of both—what I call the **early lead change.** The turn begins with a telemark and, using an early lead change, finishes with a parallel. This is a smooth, elegant turn.

Why a hybrid? Smoother lead changes, more carving, and more stability. The parallel turn finish, with uphill ski advanced, puts you in the perfect position for a telemark turn initiation with a simple change of edges. You don't have to swap feet. It's the best of both worlds, using the tele at the initiation where you need stability fore-to-aft, and the parallel at the finish where you need stability side-to-side.

Back to your practice slope. Warm up with some of your classic teles. In this maneuver your lead is changed between turns, just as you finish one and start the next. It's as though you are shuffling from turn to turn. The skis are across the fall line when you change leads.

Next, try changing the lead earlier. Start the first turn with a telemark, standing tall and steering your skis into the fall line. As your skis find the fall line, *slide the rear ski forward.* Keep it *weighted* and *edged* as long as you can, until it passes the other foot, ahead in the parallel "lead." Shift your weight to your outside ski in the parallel turn finish.

The sensation is as though you are "collecting" your skis and knees as your skis come out of the fall line. You may think of it as driving your rear thigh forward, or through, into an alpine stance. Again, keep that ski weighted until the split-second it comes under you, the transition from the tele lead to the parallel lead.

Notice in the sequence of illustrations how the telemark lead disappears and the turn is finished alpine style (see illus. 47). You check your speed facing downhill in anticipation of the next turn. With the advanced uphill ski of the parallel turn, you have the proper lead to smoothly and quickly initiate a new telemark by simply rolling your knees and edges into the fall line. There's no need for a strenuous lead change into a new tele.

With practice you will find this earlier lead transition much smoother and quicker than changing your lead between turns. It's not meant to replace the smooth, classic telemark, but rather to add another turn variation to your repertoire.

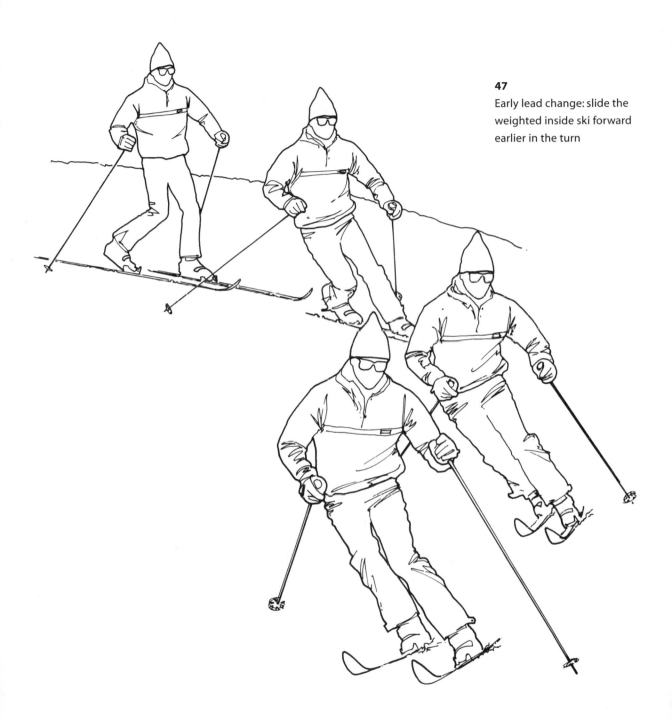

47
Early lead change: slide the
weighted inside ski forward
earlier in the turn

Skiing from the Waist Up

A number of years ago Yvon Chouinard and I traveled to Japan to ski on the island of Hokkaido. What a place to ski! Hokkaido was enjoying its usual bumper winter with an abundance of cold, fresh powder. We toured all over the island, chauffeured by a stately, elderly Japanese friend who would sneak away to soak in the nearby hot springs while we beat ourselves up on the slopes.

Skiing in Japan was a different experience. It's rare when recreational skiers in Japan venture off the piste. At the top of each lift, only a short walk would bring us to acres of virgin snow. The best slopes were serviced by odd little single chairs—the Japanese are very private people. In a chair no larger than a dinner plate for my American-sized seat, I clung to the bar, looking for more untouched terrain and those perfectly spaced Japanese trees.

I remember well an out-of-the-way little spot at the large Niseko ski area, a gully with heavy, deep snow topped with a desperate wind crust. It was difficult. If you hesitated the least bit between turns your skis wouldn't come around. Both Yvon and I became possessed with the idea of skiing this crud, caught up in the aggressive attitude it demanded. You had to plant your pole as firmly as the snow allowed and totally commit your upper body down the hill. A loud grunt was the perfect signal to begin each new arc.

Typically polite and austere, our Japanese ski partners didn't know what to think about the two Americans fanatically grunting down the desperate slope, riding up on the dinner plate, and going back again. They would follow us politely, quietly face-planting in the treacherous conditions. But finally even Japanese patience succumbed. Exasperated, they tried it, first grunting tentatively, then aggressively, as they committed their bodies to the fall line and their turning efforts began to work.

Photo on preceding page
© Scott Cramer

Up until now I haven't talked much about what to do with your body from the waist up: hands, arms, poles, and torso. I have mentioned keeping your hands in front of you and taking your eyes off of your ski tips and looking ahead. Those are the first, fundamental steps in working with your upper body.

I often see beginners struggling to turn their skis with their arms and upper body. But since skis are attached to your feet, most of the active turning comes from the waist down. That's not to say that your torso's not involved; its attitude is critical in turning your skis. But the foundation starts with the feet. Once those fundamental turning skills are acquired, then comes refining the use of the arms and torso. In advanced classes I've found that many skiers need more help with their upper body, including hands and arms, than any other part of their technique. It's something that we all continue to work on, regardless of our skiing level.

As you start on this section, be sure that you are comfortable with your feet, ankles, knees, and what you do with them. Use these exercises to set up your upper body to get even more out of your feet, knees, and skis.

ANTICIPATION

It's not easy facing down the hill on a steep slope, but you must. The attitude is called **anticipation.** It was named by the French skier Georges Joubert in reference to the torso's positioning in anticipation of the upcoming turn. Learn it well. It's an important key to all advanced skiing.

Anticipation is something that we all work on in our skiing, regardless of our level. It requires proper poling, separation of the upper and lower body, dynamic movement of the torso into the fall line—all focuses that will change you from a good skier into a great one. By facing in the right direction, your skiing will become easier, more effective, and more elegant.

Anticipation has to be developed by degrees. For the beginner, it starts with the eyes, taking them off the ski tips to look farther down the hill (see illus. 48). For the intermediate, it's pointing chest and hands down the hill. For the advanced skier, it's incorporating pole plants to "block" the torso and face the arms and shoulders down the hill. For the expert, it's fluid movement. It's an attitude of the upper body that, when combined with momentum, becomes total freedom—an independent upper body confidently floating toward the next turn while the skis cross under, turning freely back and forth. The torso is independent of the legs, moving as though it were joined only by a ball-and-socket or universal joint. Anticipation is an *attitude*, not a twisting,

48
Look farther
down the hill

of the torso. It's as simple as where you are looking, where you are going.

To achieve this freedom, expert skiers combine all of the basic points of anticipation. They use their eyes, torso, arms, shoulders, and pole plants together. Each one of these elements is important from the beginning. Experts always go back to them. They use them as a way to cure bad habits or as a focal point for a difficult descent.

FOCAL POINTS

The upper body reflects a skier's "attitude" on skis. Timid skiers may stand very square over their skis, afraid to face the fall line. Defensive skiers even lean and twist up the hill to avoid the fall line.

What you are *thinking* about when you ski can really affect the attitude of your upper body. Below, I've listed a few focal points that I use to get my upper body facing and floating down the fall line.

- Think of your shoulders as an artificial horizon on the instrument panel of an airplane. Try to keep that artificial horizon level with the horizon of the snow slope.

- Think of your chest as having a headlight (see illus. 49). Pick a target down the hill in the fall line and point that light at the target. As you make turns, keep your light on the target without veering from side to side.

49
Think of your shoulders as an artificial horizon; think of your chest as having a headlight

50

Face the outside
of the turn

- Think of facing the *outside* of the turn—down the hill—rather than the inside (see illus. 50). That means that if you are turning right, try to face the outside of that turn: left. That will get you facing down the hill.
- Think of your navel as though it has a string running from it. As you link your turns, imagine someone pulling you down the hill with that string. Let the string pull you; don't pull against it. The feeling, the focus, is *weightlessness* as you allow gravity's string to pull you down the fall line. Moving this direction is the *three-dimensional* movement that I've talked about—not just standing up vertically, but *extending* and moving the body down the hill.

These different focal points will help you with your upper body's attitude and the flow of your turns. Be sure to use them *one at a time*; more than one is too confusing.

POLING

Back in the old days skiers used one pole like an outrigger, leaning on it for balance and dragging it between their legs as a brake. Then for about eighty years or so, skiers skied with two poles. Today, Norwegians, especially, have reintroduced their heritage and often practice with one pole. Other countries influenced by the Norwegians have caught on to one pole, too. It's a fun thing to try, although in this book I'm going to stick with two poles, the most practical arrangement for propulsion and timing.

To be used properly, your poles must be the right length. For downhill skiing, whether alpine or telemark, alpine-length poles are the best choice. When touring, your poles should be longer for additional "push" on uphills and flats.

An excellent solution for backcountry skiing, where the terrain goes both up and down, is a pair of adjustable poles that telescope from alpine to nordic touring length. You can adjust them long on the flats and uphills, short on the downhills, and two different lengths on long traverses.

Poles and Balance

Once you get your pole length straightened out, specific poling exercises can improve your technique. You can eliminate your dependence on poles for balance and learn to use them primarily for *timing* and *body position*.

Here is an old alpine exercise especially useful for tele skiers who depend on their poles for balance: hold your poles horizontally across your body (see illus. 51). In each hand you will have the grip of one pole and the shaft of the other. Hold them with your arms relaxed in front of your chest. Try to keep the poles level with your shoulders. Think of the poles as a carpenter's level, and try to keep the middle bubble even with the snow's horizon.

Removing the crutch of your poles can make you painfully conscious of bad habits. For instance, many telemark skiers have a habit of leaning on their uphill pole. They use a rapid uphill pole plant for balance at the finish of each turn and for propulsion into the next. Once that pole is gone, their pole-check becomes a butt-check. If you feel that without your poles you are falling uphill too much, put more weight on your back foot in the little-toe area at each turn's finish, and don't lean into the hill.

Note: Don't carry your car keys in your back pocket.

51
Hold your poles
horizontally across
your body

Once you feel comfortable linking tele or parallel turns without poles, you can let the poles drop to a normal position. Keep your hands in the same spot as when holding your poles across your body—within your peripheral vision. You don't need to plant the poles; simply find a comfortable position for your hands, poles pointing behind you.

Poles and Timing

Poles are put to good use by *timing* your turns. A proper pole plant stores energy and regulates the release of that energy into the next turn.

Practice turn timing. Tap the snow lightly with the downhill pole before you start each turn. Then turn your skis around the hole you've made in the snow. Think *tap, turn, tap, turn, tap, turn* (see illus. 52). Plant only the

52
Think "tap, turn, tap, turn, . . . "

downhill pole for each new turn. Planting the downhill (inside) pole may be contrary to some region's telemark dogma, but double poling or planting only the uphill pole only reinforces bad habits.

Uphill pole plants lean and rotate your body uphill into the slope—the wrong way to be facing. Some skiers use double pole plants for security in that unstable transition between turns. For some quick-footed skiers these pole plants work—especially when making tight turns in big, steep bumps. But for others this habit squares the body on the skis so that quick turning requires propulsion off the two planted poles—a difficult feat in soft snow. That's why we'll practice single pole plants.

Remember when practicing your poling that it requires *timing*—an elusive skill dependent on feel and image rather than conscious thought. If you get confused while practicing this skill, do something else. Watch good alpine skiers and imitate their poling movements. Follow a good skier, planting your pole in the same spots that he or she plants and turning your skis in the same tracks. *Don't think.* Try to *see* and *feel*.

Different Poling for Different Turns

Watch good alpine skiers and you will notice that their hands stay comfortable and controlled. Hands help create the right attitude for the rest of the body. Hold your arms comfortably flexed, not outstretched, keeping your hands in front of you in the periphery of your vision (not down by your hips).

When cruising and making larger-radius turns, a pole plant is used primarily to position your body and signal the edge change for the next turn. There is a relaxed, flowing transition between turns. You swing the pole forward for a gentle pole "touch" as you *rise up* into the new arc (see illus. 52). With these big turns you're probably skiing fast, so the pole plant should be gentle, not a firm sting or gouge that might slow you down. These are the easiest pole plants to mimic and learn. It's the short-radius pole plant that usually needs more attention.

In short-radius turns, especially on steeper terrain, you want to *decelerate*, not *accelerate*. Applied in the split-second transition between quick turns, the pole plant becomes a *braking* technique. It is firm and decisive at the end of the downward movement of your body as you finish the turn and begin the next. It's a *sting* of your pole tip and ski edges *at the same time*: simultaneously stinging the snow with edges and the downhill pole before moving into the new turn. It feels quick and aggressive (see illus. 53).

53

The short-radius
pole plant in an
aggressive sting

To get your pole forward in time for this sting, you'll have to swing it forward. Usually your "pole swing" matches your turn radius; in the case of the short-radius turn, it's quicker and more pronounced. The pole swing is a subtle movement at the wrist (see illus. 54).

Your pole plant sets you up for short-radius turns. It's a move crucial to making the skis come around easily in otherwise difficult snow. With the

54
Your pole swing should
match the radius of your turn;
a subtle move of the wrist

pole basket planted down the hill, the planted pole pushes back against your arm and shoulder and forces your upper body to face downhill. The body twist created by this "blocking" movement stores energy in contracted and stretched muscle groups. When you release this energy into the next turn, your skis are launched into the arc with minimal effort. Whether in heavy crud or light powder, it's the best trick for rhythmic, well-linked turns.

Think of your poling as though you are opening a door for your torso to move through. The door opens into the next turn (see illus. 54 and 55). In short turns, that means the door opens directly down the hill—plant your pole downhill, below the boot. In longer turns, the pole plant is more across the hill. Plant the pole more ahead, toward the ski tip.

For some skiers, this idea of *where* to plant the pole is easiest. Notice where the pole is planted in the short-radius turns in the last illustration. The skier's pole is planted clear back by the heel of the boot—between the heel and the fall line (see illus. 55). This helps frame the door for the next

55

The pole plant opens the door down the hill (parallel turn)

turn. Plant the pole farther back toward the heel for short turns, farther ahead toward the ski tip for longer turns.

A different image will help prevent your hands from dropping behind—a common error that leans you into the hill. Once you plant your pole, focus on punching the poling hand forward and "over" the pole. On steeps, exaggerate this idea, punching your poling (downhill) and uphill hands down the hill. Resist the temptation to let your hands—especially your uphill hand—fall behind or drop low by your hip. Keep your hands moving *forward*, down the fall line.

Poling in Crud

Subtle hand movements can work wonders to bring your skis around in thick conditions. I mentioned earlier that the inside hand on the planted pole moves *forward*, over the pole. The outside (uphill) hand will also aid your turning—especially in difficult snow.

Try it in crud: as you move aggressively into a telemark or parallel turn, throw your outside hand sharply *forward*, down the hill. See in the illustration how the inside pole is planted while the outside hand is moving up and forward (see illus. 56).

56
Punch your outside hand forward as you plant your pole

Remember that this is an exaggeration to magnify your movements in difficult snow, where it works great. It is unnecessary on buffed piste.

Inside hand, outside hand. You can't think about it all at once. As I mentioned before, when you get confused, don't think about anything. Poling is mostly a matter of timing, a technique that is easier to ape than describe. Find a good alpine skier whose moves you can mimic.

CROSSOVER

Momentum. Flowing with gravity. That's the sign of a true expert, the skier who seems to move effortlessly down the steepest slopes in perfect control.

Appearances are deceiving. Watch really good skiers making short turns down some steep, narrow path and it will look as though their upper body is completely quiet, motionless. It's no wonder that instructors teach and students construe the torso's attitude as a *position*. It's so calm it looks almost static. But don't be fooled by that steadfast appearance. Like your feet, the torso is *alive*, moving aggressively toward the next turn. The trunk isn't behind, following the legs. It's not rotating side to side. It's not just on top of the legs. It's *leading*, moving down the hill in a much straighter line than the skis.

This concept is a much more advanced form of anticipation. The point is, this anticipation isn't just a static position, facing down the hill. All of my focuses and exercises are to get you facing the right direction, but the end goal is dynamic and fluid. Notice how, in illustration 57, the upper body follows a much straighter line than that of the skis? Like the track that your skis follow, this body line varies according to your turn radius. Usually, the tighter the turn radius, the straighter the line your body will take. In short-radius turns there's simply no time for your heavy torso to follow the serpentine path of your skis.

Most ski instructors call this **crossover:** the upper body crosses over the skis; or you can look at it as **crossunder:** as your torso floats aggressively down the fall line, your skis swing back and forth underneath.

Following such a line with the torso requires aggressive movement down the hill. While your skis are snaking back and forth under that "floating" trunk, your stomach, back, and buttocks are stretching and contracting, storing and releasing energy into each successive turn. It's a workout. There's nothing quiet or static about it.

Try an exercise that helps crossover in medium-to-long turns: moving your torso into each new turn sooner, while your skis are finishing the last turn. It's a very dynamic feeling, as your skis race in one direction across the hill while you commit your upper body to the opposite direction, into the next turn.

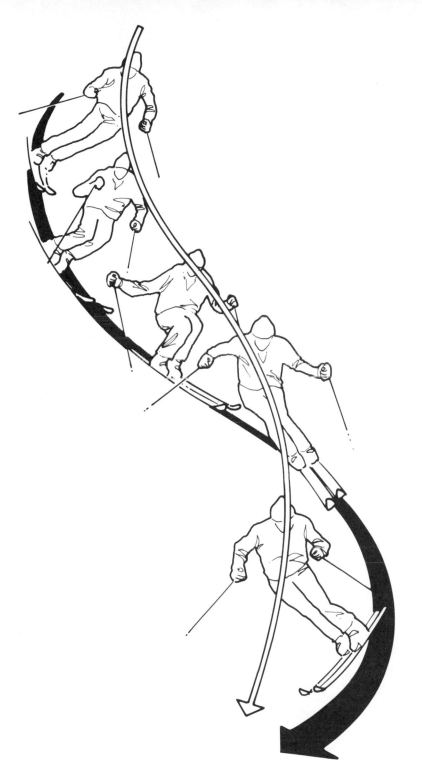

57
The line followed by the
upper body is much
straighter than the line
of the skis

On your practice slope, as your skis come across the slope toward the finish of a turn, plant your downhill pole and move your *whole torso toward a new turn* (see illus. 58). Your skis will go one way while your upper body

58
Move toward the
new turn as you
plant your pole

moves the other. It seems unlikely, but your skis miraculously snap around, finishing the last turn crisply and rebounding toward the new one. It's a similar feeling to the "stepping on the uphill ski earlier" that we did in Advanced Parallel Tips.

You might feel as though your torso leads dangerously beyond a balanced position. The payoff is that your skis seem to flatten and turn automatically. This is what we're all after.

When telemarking with this focus you'll develop a "wind-up" effect, twisting the body like a spring, storing energy to release and snap you into the next turn (refer back to illus. 54). In parallel turns you will feel your weight shift to the uphill ski before the ski is steered into a new turn.

OK, try another focus, this time for short-radius turns. Remember earlier when I said to think of a string in your navel, pulling you down the fall line with each turn? Now try moving *ahead* of the string, keeping it slack: rather than being pulled along, be more proactive and move your belly button directly down the fall line into each new turn. Don't hold back; move that belly button straight down the hill. It's the same idea: moving the torso dangerously ahead of everything else.

Parallel or telemark, the fluid movements that come from these exercises preserve the momentum of the upper body rather than slowing it. In parallel turns, they go hand-in-hand with the exercises that we've worked on throughout this book—especially pointing your knees. In telemarks, they go hand-in-hand with the early lead change. In either kind of turn, the feeling of a weightless body that isn't resisting the pull of gravity is one of the most elegant sensations of descent on skis.

Skiing on One Ski

~

By the side of the tracks, snow monkeys peered into the train, envious as we munched away at the contents of our bento boxes. The little cog train wound its way into the Japanese Alps toward Shiga Kogen. Along the way, little one-lift ski areas with blown snow were covered with acres of antlike skiers. Our buddies from Tokyo met us at the station after the long ride and ushered us off to the evening's festivities.

I've never understood how, in a culture as reserved as the Japanese, party goers can politely drink until they fall over. This instance was a pre-race meeting of the Japanese Telemark Association. Years ago on our first trip, this group had consisted of a few crusty old backcountry skiers and Eiger climbers with missing fingers, drinking ceremoniously through the night. It was now a rowdy bunch of pumped-up racers. There was a hysterical beer-swilling contest, prizes, awards, and, of course, complimentary bottles of Wild Turkey (a race sponsor) for dignitaries. I killed a potted plant with my bottle.

The next morning, while the race was getting organized, Yvon Chouinard, our buddy Fuji, and I went out for a little powder exploration. As usual in Japan, no one was skiing off-piste. Everyone was too polite to tell us not to go. Within 2 hours Y.C. and I knew the trees better than the ski patrol. It was cool skiing: 18 inches or so on a rock-hard rain crust. At the finish of each powder turn, with a little oomph, you could hit the crust and get a great slalom-type rebound into the next face shot. Powder/trees/slalom/HAI!

We'd poached long enough and headed for the race course. The course had two huge pro jumps that looked like auto-exhibit podiums at a car show. Huge. I laughed at the folly of telemark racing—"Stupid racers . . . who would want to fly off of that thing onto a rock-hard landing?" Ten seconds later, Yamura-san skied up and said that I was to fore-run the race. At least 200 people would be watching and, of course, I was a famous telemark skier and would do well and not lose face. Oh, my head.

Photo on preceding page
© Mark Shapiro

▲   165

Numerous turns into it, trying to carry maximum speed, I gritted my teeth and tried to suck up the huge jump. Of course, I was going way too fast and, at the lip, popped so much air that I flew over the next gate, flag at my ankles. I touched down and desperately pulled off a couple of white-knuckled alpine turns before the finish. The crowd went wild, thinking that "Papaka"-san had popped air and arced a few alpine carves not out of desperation, but as a demonstration.

In the race that followed, that jump caused a lot of carnage. Awards were presented for the most air, the most air upside down, and the most desperate groin-tweaking recovery. No one lost face.

Once again in the festive mode, my hosts asked me to do a clinic. I sneaked off with a bunch of the racers on one of the many bulletproof trails. They were all superb piste skiers. Every exercise, every turn that I demonstrated, they performed flawlessly, the first time, better than I could. Wanting to show them something new, I racked my brain for something that they couldn't do.

The light went on: skiing on one ski. These guys were all used to steppy, sequential racing arcs. I figured that they weren't likely to have been practicing on one ski.

A chorus of polite Japanese guttural "auhoouhooos" accompanied me as I skied down through the group, demonstrating short-radius turns on one foot. Eyes got very big. I pantomimed that they should try; the video rolled, cameras clicked, and the giggling started.

Success.

My Japanese class eventually caught on, and they were fascinated how this exercise emphasized the weight and edge on what normally would be their inside ski for half of their turns. Skiing on one ski is difficult. It's an excellent exercise for edging, using the inside ski and balance maneuvers that come in handy with the unexpected.

Try it. Pick a soft, easy slope, stand on your stronger leg, and try to make a few lefts and rights on that stronger side. Hold the other ski up off of the snow (see illus. 59). I can't give you much more description. You'll have to try.

Do you find yourself lurching around to get that ski to turn on its outside edge? There is a trick: your *ankle*. Give it your undivided attention. *Flex your ankle* from the inside corner of your boot (as in a normal parallel turn), to the outside corner of your boot to make that trickier uphill turn (see "The Inside Corner" in Advanced Parallel Tips). You should feel the outside edge under the little-toe side of your foot.

Practice these turns until you can do them on both sides. Now, put both feet on the ground and see what happens. Do you feel how independent your feet are, how "mobile" you've become? Feel that uphill edge? Are you more confident with the inside ski?

Once you get the hang of it, your feet become much more independent. You'll find that using that ankle to edge your uphill ski improves the edging of the downhill one. You'll find that you can edge your back (uphill) ski better in a telemark. The end result is more carve, less skid.

59
Skiing on one ski: hold your
other ski off the snow

Powder

Slow-motion grace, effortless movement. Cold, light snow bubbling over my head and pressing sensuously against my body. That's what I feel when I hear the word *powder*.

The locals wait for it. Tentative skiers avoid it. It isn't always effortless, but it's ultimate.

Powder skiing requires proper technique. The snow changes frequently from turn to turn. It weighs heavily on your skis when the sun beats down. It grows dense and perilous with pounding wind.

The resistance of powder snow can give you a false sense of security. You feel as though you don't have to finish your turns because the snow slows you down. But you'll find that as the terrain steepens you'd better finish your turns round and controlled or you're quickly out of control; and unlike on a groomed slope, you can't simply steer your skis sideways to scrape off speed, unless you want to head-plant. You must control your speed with the *arc* of your turn, flexing your skis from the very start to the very finish of each turn. Learn to turn your skis in round, complete arcs and you'll have the technique for the ultimate powder runs, the real steep and deep.

STARTING OUT IN POWDER

Most skiers have so little opportunity to ski powder that it takes them years to learn how. Unless you live at one of a handful of those legendary deep-snow areas, there is too little of it for consistent practice. There are, however, a number of points of focus that with practice will help you hone your powder skiing as quickly as possible. These ideas have been covered before, and they apply to both parallel and telemark skiers.

- Get the feel of equal weight distribution between your skis.
- Strive for equal edging as well as equal weight.
- Use your entire range of motion, with a strong emphasis on extension and flexion of the legs.

Photo on preceding page
© Brian Litz

- Aggressively move your body down the hill toward the next turn. This is the ultimate move that is a key to expert powder skiing.

I'll start with the first idea. It's worth noting for this practice that even if you are an expert piste skier it's best when practicing powder technique to stay clear of rocks and trees. Find a gentle, open slope—ideally one that is covered with a blanket of light, fresh snow. Start by practicing straight running. Once you build a little speed, shift your weight from one ski to another. Quickly you will feel how weight is best distributed between your feet. (In a parallel it's even, like a telemark.) Make some straight runs in the flats and get the feeling of this equal distribution.

Now, still without turning, start moving up and down. You can practice this with your feet in a parallel position or by switching tele leads if you're working on your teles. You should use a bouncing rhythm, standing tall and sinking, extending and flexing. If you're tele skiing, think of sinking *between* your feet. This is a good way to start any powder run, feeling the snow for its resistance and consistency.

Are you comfortable with your weight distribution? Then try a turn: while rising (tele or parallel), press hard on your feet and twist them into a turn. Some describe this as "grinding" their heels (and forefoot in a tele) into the turn. Rise with your body, pressing as you twist your feet, grinding into the cold, light snow. It's easiest to practice one turn at a time, turning into the hill to a stop. Can you feel how your skis flex into an arc, scribing a turn?

Notice the difference in your footwork between parallels and teles: in a parallel stance you're pushing both of your heels away from you evenly; in a telemark you're grinding on the inside heel of your front foot and on the ball of the rear foot (little-toe side). For telemark skiers the rear ski is crucial, so be conscious of exerting plenty of weight on that back ski. Use the early edging and steering motions I described in Advanced Telemark Tips.

To link your turns you will have to add the other half to the extension of your legs: a flexion, a sinking motion, relaxing and contracting your legs as you finish each turn. It makes sense. Without sinking, you can't rise again into another arc. Extension and flexion is the distinctive up-and-down technique you see in the films—skiers elegantly using both ends of their range of motion, high and low.

Rise sharply and press your feet away from you to initiate either a telemark or a parallel turn. As your skis come out of the fall line, sink and twist your feet into the turn finish. You won't have to try very hard. The resistance of the snow will help finish your turn, pulling your skis further around as you twist your feet, pushing them up and flexing your legs as the pressure builds under your skis. Don't resist; relax your legs as this pressure builds, letting the snow do the work for you. This automatic flexion, and letting the snow do the pushing, is why powder skiers call their favorite turns "effortless."

Gain some speed on your gentle slope, rising and pressing with your feet to start the turns, sinking as you turn your feet into the finish. When you feel the bouncy rhythm, add a pole plant at the lowest point of each bounce. This will punctuate each turn, setting you up for a rise into your next one. In this case it's OK—in fact it's best—to exaggerate the up-and-down and pole-plant punctuation.

DEALING WITH THE STEEP AND DEEP

So what about the steep and deep we hear so much about? There are tricks for teles or parallel turns that you should always keep available:

- Reread the paragraph above about rhythm and bounce. Try to see that up- and down rhythm in your mind's eye. Watch Warren Miller movies, ski-school videos, cable TV, and good skiers under the lift. Use any visual trick that gives you an image of that loose, bouncy rhythm.
- Face down the hill. I know I've said it many times, but you really need to do it here. Face those arms, chest, and navel right down the hill as though you're perfectly confident that your turns will happen. Telemark skiers have to exaggerate this body twist because it's much harder to face the fall line with the rotated hip of the telemark.
- Exaggerate your flexion and extension. At this stage it will feel like an up-and-down movement. Stand taller and sink lower than you think is possible. Rise sharply to emphasize the "pressing away" of your feet, flexing your skis as soon as you begin the arc. Compared with how you feel during your piste turns, you will feel like you are rising earlier in the turn and sinking longer (see illus. 60).
- Sharply raise your outside hand up and forward as you rise, in order to emphasize your body's extension.
- Don't lean in. Leaning into the hill is the nemesis of powder skiers.
- Practice garlands on steeper slopes, turning into the hill to a stop.
- Practice your turns in both directions. Exaggerate that early extension of your feet into the turns, then sink as your skis come out of the fall line.

60
Exaggerate your flexion and extension in powder

FALL-LINE TURNS

The crux on the steeps certainly isn't turning into the hill to a stop. It's turning *into the fall line*. This time we'll link some turns.

As your skis come out of the fall line and you feel the resistance of the snow slowing you down, *relax your legs*. Let the snow push your feet up into the turn finish. The powder's resistance will help you sink through the turn and push your feet upward to automatically flex your legs (refer back to illus. 60).

As the snow pushes your skis up and around, it packs into a platform under your feet. Reach down the fall line and plant your pole to signal the next turn. At the split-second that you plant that pole, edge both skis sharply—imagine a gentle *sting* with the pole plant and edges. Now you're committed. Keeping your legs relaxed, "roll" your skis off the platform and into the next turn.

Parallel skiers should think of rolling both skis in the parallel position. Tele skiers should think of rolling and switching leads. I like to think of starting a turn by rolling onto the inside edge of my new back foot—the "Making Smoother Turns" exercise that we worked on earlier in the chapter Advanced Parallel Tips. Whether you're doing a parallel or a tele, as your skis roll toward the fall line, *move your body aggressively into the next turn*: extend your legs, rise sharply, and raise your outside hand to emphasize the extension.

As your skis drop off the platform they'll be very light. Try to make them heavier with your extension and bend them into an arc. Think "heavy feet." Think about keeping them deep in the snow. "Reach" down the hill with your feet. You'll know it the moment you feel it—that weightlessness as your skis drop off the platform and your body's complete extension as your feet reach for the snow below.

WEIGHT DISTRIBUTION AND OTHER FOCAL POINTS

A bad habit that is hard to break is "sitting back." Once you do that it's too easy to get stuck there in the "back seat." You simply don't have to sit back in powder to keep your tips up. In parallel turns I like to emphasize the weight on the rear two-thirds of my foot from the arch back. In tele turning I emphasize the weight *between* my feet, with plenty of rear-foot pressure.

Just as important as fore-to-aft weight distribution in powder is your weight distribution from side-to-side. In deep snow parallel skiers weight and edge *both* skis much more evenly than on packed slopes. Many refer to this equal weighting as "skiing two skis as one" (see illus. 61). Telemark skiers weight and edge both skis, too (see illus. 62). If you don't weight *and* edge both skis you will have all sorts of problems: the splits, crossed tips, or high-speed figure-elevens. If you step your turns around you'll have similar troubles. Beware: You must weight and edge both of your skis *simultaneously* as you initiate each turn. For me, the best focus is the one mentioned earlier in this section and earlier in the book in both Advanced Telemark Tips and Advanced Parallel Tips: think of the inside (uphill) edge of your rear ski as the first thing to touch the snow.

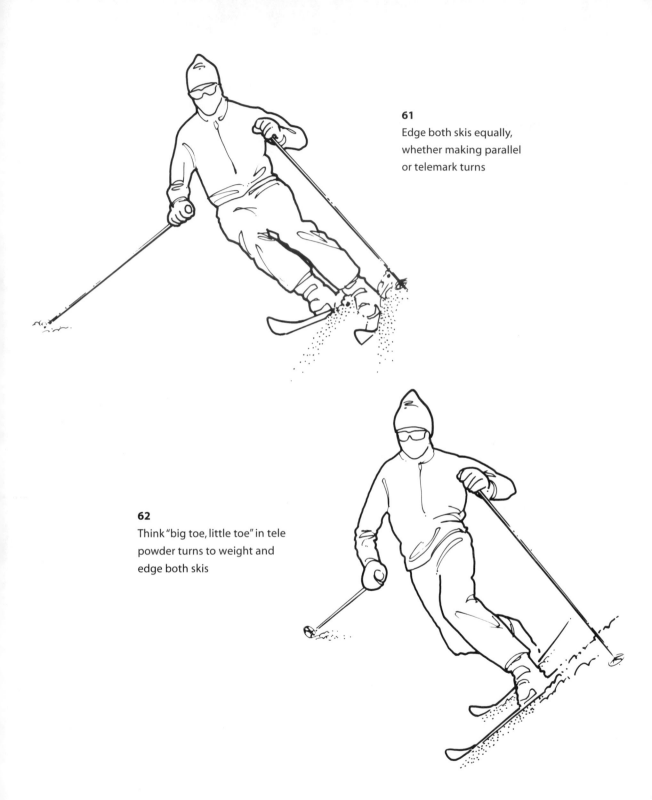

61
Edge both skis equally,
whether making parallel
or telemark turns

62
Think "big toe, little toe" in tele
powder turns to weight and
edge both skis

Notice how I keep talking about parallel turns? Yes, free-heel parallels are possible in powder. Sure, it's intimidating to try to turn in deep snow without sticking that leading ski ahead for security. But if you want to practice parallels, just find good powder that's not too deep or grabby, and weight both skis equally. Try to make as many parallel turns as you can, and when you get in trouble drop into a tele. You'll soon find that you won't have to make that survival tele. You'll be looking for opportunities to powder parallel.

A good exercise to review if you're working on parallel turns is the "Focus on Your Inside Knee" exercise in the Advanced Parallel Tips that helps you edge both skis equally. (You might think of it as tipping over the skis since you really aren't edging into a hard surface.) As you tip (edge) your skis into each new turn, focus on *pointing your inside knee in this new turning direction.*

Telemarkers can weight both skis evenly by emphasizing pressure on the back foot. Tuck your rear leg snugly under you. Don't let it trail behind. Be sure to edge both skis simultaneously, moving onto the ball of your rear foot (little-toe side) at the same time—or even earlier—that you pressure the big-toe side of your front foot. Yeah, it's "big toe, little toe" again (refer back to illus. 62). It will help to go back to the Advanced Telemark Tips chapter to review these ideas.

Last, but by no means least, once you're more comfortable with the idea of powder and getting your skis around in it, work on your anticipation. As I said before, it's not just a static facing of the torso down the hill but a dynamic movement of the body into the next turn. At first it's hard to make this aggressive move in powder. Your natural reaction is to rotate defensively, keeping your upper body in the *last* turn rather than moving it into the next one. It feels secure. But what have you got to lose? The snow's soft, and it's easy to stop.

Try it. Find a slope with soft, forgiving snow, tighten your cuffs and zippers, put on your hat, and go for it. Make yourself move your body into the next turn. Plant your pole as a signal, and move your navel aggressively down the hill into the next turn. *Go for it.* Try the emphasis I used in Skiing from the Waist Up: as your skis come across the hill to finish the last turn, move your upper body in the *opposite* direction. Keep trying and you'll feel it.

Ah, that weightless feeling of moving your body confidently down the hill toward the fall line. Once you experience that sensation, you will have opened the door to truly fun powder skiing.

Crud Skiing

Most skiers avoid difficult snow. It hurts their knees and their egos. Then there are some like a Swiss friend of mine who claims, "There is no bad snow, just bad skiers." Bull. There is plenty of bad snow. But just because it's bad, just because it's difficult, doesn't mean it's not skiable. "Survival" skiing can provide some of the most rewarding turning there is.

HOP AND HOPE

In soft crud I try to keep my skis in the snow as much as possible and ski it like powder, using an exaggerated flexion and extension of my legs. Terrain allowing, I'll use larger-radius turns; speed helps you plow through heavy snow. If it's steeper, I'll use short-radius turns, but I still *try to keep the skis in the snow*. I'm airborne in the fall line, but it's because of the steepness and my skis' rebound, not because I'm jumping them around.

Jump turns are not a substitute for carving skis. In fact, if you become too dependent on them, you'll lose the smooth control in a carve that is critical for edge hold on hard snow and for smooth arcs in powder. First learn to arc, saving the jump for when you really need it.

When is that? When the snow is desperate, I do choose to leap and land (hop and hope). What's desperate? Refrozen crud, breakable crust, snow that is just too unpredictable or too dangerous to push through. In those situations, especially with free heels, you are wise to get out of the snow and into the air. Some prefer telemark jump turns; personally I find the "collected" position of the parallel turn the most effective for leaping and landing.

On steeper terrain, jump turns aren't difficult; in fact, steepness helps get your skis airborne. The trick to jump turns is timing—much like good poling technique. It's a huge help if you can find a good skier to mimic down the hill.

Photo on preceding page
© Scott Cramer

PARALLEL JUMP TURNS

Here is the "sequence of events" for parallel jump turns:

- Traverse to gain speed with skis parallel.
- Anticipate the upcoming turn, facing *directly* down the fall line.
- Set your uphill edges to make a platform and *aggressively* plant your pole down the hill.
- Grunt out loud, pushing up hard off of the platform and *sharply moving your outside arm down the hill.*
- Suck up your legs, cranking your skis around. Be sure to point your inside knee into the new turn.
- Land with your skis parallel and traverse to the next spot where you want to turn.

Don't worry if you didn't get all of that because I'm going to repeat it. Note that to practice jump turns you should thoroughly understand the chapter on Skiing from the Waist Up. You will need many of the same ideas—skiing tough conditions is where clean technique and good body position really count. Difficult snow is like a magnifier. It emphasizes each unnecessary little quirk in your technique and uses each one against you. You must go back to the basics: shoulders facing down the hill, hands held ahead, pole plants properly timed, and skillful edging.

It's easiest to practice crud turns one at a time. It helps if the slope is a little steeper because your skis are automatically on edge. If you make one turn at a time you can make one turn, regain your composure in a traverse, then make another turn. When making one turn at a time, however, you can't use the energy stored from the finish of the last turn to snap into the next. You'll need a "pre-turn" to set you up for each complete turn: you need to execute a strong sinking, edging, and steering motion before you push off into the new turn. That's the step above that combines the aggressive pole plant and edge set.

OK, we're on the slope. I'll break it down again. Try seeing these moves in your mind's eye:

- Get a bit of speed up and then sink quickly—sink, steer uphill, and edge *both* skis—planting your pole aggressively as you do so (see the top figure in illus. 63).
- Now, extend your legs and stand up abruptly. Push off that platform with *both* feet and launch your body into the air. *Raise your outside arm sharply* to help give yourself more lift. Point your inside knee into the

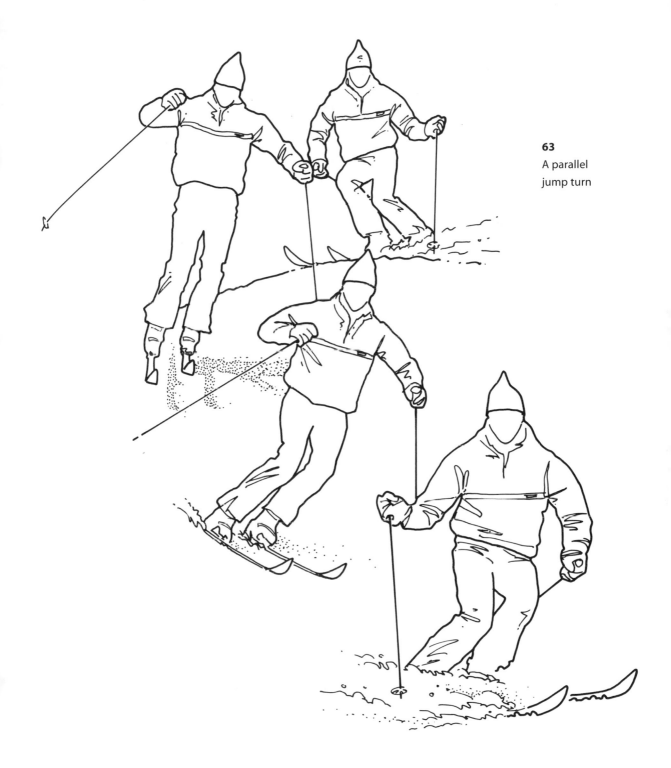

63
A parallel
jump turn

new turn. You can see that move in the second figure of the parallel jump turn illustration.

- Think of your legs as landing gear. As your skis lighten toward the end of your body's upward extension, lengthen your air time by "bringing up the landing gear." Suck up your legs and bring them out of the snow. With your legs contracted and skis pulled upward, you are now free of whatever catchy snow you are trying to avoid. Point your skis in the desired direction and make your turn in midair.
- Once your skis are turned, lower your landing gear and finish your turn. Reach for the snow with your legs extended so you can absorb the shock as you land. Landing and absorbing with *both* of your legs will store energy for your next leap.

To execute jump turns you must use a strong pole plant. If you plant your pole in the right place at the right time, the wound-up energy in your abdomen and torso will do most of the turning for you. Sound familiar? You must anticipate and be totally committed to each upcoming turn, facing directly down the fall line. Plant your pole in the fall line directly below your boots—clear back by your heel if the slope is steep—not forward toward your tips. This pole-plant position forces your torso to face down the hill and increases the "wind-up" effect. Note the strong pole plants of the first and last figures in the illustration.

The pole plant is a firm, decisive sting that punctuates the end of each turn and the start of the next. Brace your torso with the pole. Your torso will want to rotate through the turn finish, but poling stops this movement and stores the energy in the muscles of your back and abdomen. As you leap up and bring your skis out of the snow, this stored muscular energy launches your skis into the next turn.

TELEMARK JUMP TURNS

In many situations I use parallel jump turns. But if advanced parallel turns aren't in your bag of tricks yet, or if you prefer telemarks, you will want to practice jump-tele turns (see illus. 64). If you are a parallel skier, tele turns will be fun to do for a change. The timing, pole plant, and anticipatory moves of teles are the same as in parallel turns.

The big difference that I find between jump teles and jump parallels is in getting my hips around from one tele to the next while in midair. It takes a lot of *punch*.

Here's the sequence using the classic telemark lead change:

- Traverse in a telemark position, downhill foot advanced.
- Sink and edge—big toe, little toe—to make a pre-turn, anticipating with your torso and planting your pole firmly.
- Push up hard on both feet, raise your outside arm, and move your body into the fall line. Take advantage of the lightening of your skis from your sharp upward movement and change leads by dropping your new inside ski/foot *back*.
- Continue to lighten your skis by sucking up your "landing gear"; turn your airborne skis where you want to go.
- Land in the next tele, ready for your traverse and another turn.

64
A jump-tele turn

In some snow I prefer using the telemark **early lead change** (see the chapter More Free-heel Turns) so that I can make the pre-turn in a stable parallel position. Plus, when finishing in a parallel turn you already have the correct lead for initiating the next tele. The chief difference between this and the classic lead change is in the traverse-and-turn initiation:

- Make the initial traverse in a *parallel stance*. When you sink and edge for your pre-turn, make sure your skis are in a parallel turn finish rather than a tele.
- Push off as in a parallel jump turn, raising your outside arm.
- Once your body is tall, suck your legs up and turn your skis, landing in a tele.
- Tele-turn out of the fall line, quickly sliding the uphill ski forward into a parallel position for your next parallel pre-turn.

It's optimistic to think that you can jump right into difficult snow and practice linked short turns. First practice the proper techniques in an easier situation, not necessarily on groomed conditions but in a better exposure, one with less wind deposition and not so steep. Learn the sensations in this environment. When you jump into harder snow, imagine yourself making and feeling the same moves as you did in practice.

Practice the turns one at a time as I have described them. This makes the fall line less intimidating. As your confidence grows, try eliminating the traverse altogether. Jump from one turn to another with a "fall-line attitude." At first it's strenuous, but when you get the hang of it you will be able to use the snap in your skis to take much of the effort out of your jump.

Easy to say, I know. With practice, you will find turns of this kind quite easy. Learn the timing, visualize it in your mind's eye, and ski the image that you "see."

Photo on following page © Ace Kvale

Slush

I only saw Robert's fall out of the corner of my eye. Hearing an unsettling crashing noise, I turned around to see him twisted into an improbable contortion, one of his skis pointed the wrong direction. His face was covered with blood. Immediately the image of an open fracture crossed my mind: stabilize the victim, shock, helicopters. All unsavory. I climbed back through the bottomless mashed potatoes as quickly as I could, relieved to see that his ski was off, with his foot pointing in a normal direction—not the skis'. The blood was a minor face wound, one of those that bleeds like crazy. Robert had carved a turn with the bridge of his prominent Gallic nose. It was nothing serious, just two weeks back at work of: "What happened to you?"

The skiing down to Zermatt on the lower Tiefmatten glacier that day was way beyond crud. Up high on the Col de Valpelline it had been great, even firm, with several thousand feet of silky corn. But the last kilometer it was no-man's land. You would be sliding along carefully, wet snow sucking at your ski bases, and then suddenly drop down toward the ground—except there was no ground underneath. We struggled through these final turns of the glacier covered with meters of unconsolidated slop.

I'm not wild about sloppy spring skiing. I live where skiing lasts into late spring/early summer. Yet as the season winds down and the temperature warms up, I usually confine my skiing to peak climbs. I love the sunrise in those early morning hours, crunch-crunching up the climb on firmly frozen firn that, after a thermos of tea on top, transforms to silky corn for the descent.

Once it turns to wet slop, I go home and ride my bike.

If you don't particularly want to ski slush, often all you need to do is get out of bed an hour earlier. But it's not always that simple. In backcountry skiing and ski mountaineering, you don't always have that luxury. It's common to have several climbs and descents through the day, the firm base turning to bottomless slush before you're done. Or you might like slop—or need to ski

Photo on preceding page
© Brian Litz

it to get in position to watch the bikini contest. So it's not a bad idea to have a few technical tricks in your pocket as well as proper ski preparation in anticipation of a melt-down.

PREPARE YOUR SKIS FOR SLUSH

Structure, the surface treatment given to your skis' polyethylene base, is most important. The structure's **pattern,** which is cut into the base, helps channel water to break suction between the snow and the ski. If you anticipate slop, you want to structure and wax your skis aggressively for the wettest snow.

Skis glide on a thin layer of water at all temperatures. For dry snow you use a finer structure, with tiny grooves in a regular pattern on the base's surface. This pattern is fine because it is dealing with a very thin layer of water on an almost microscopic level. A wet snow structure is much more aggressive, with obvious grooves. Like a car tire designed to channel rainwater away from the tire's contact surface, these grooves channel water and break up the suction between the base and saturated snow. A wet-snow structure will eliminate a lot of the nose-smashing "sucky" feeling that yanks your skis back while everything else continues ahead.

Any good ski-tuning shop can give your skis a wet-snow structure when you get them tuned. Every spring I have my backcountry skis stone-ground with this structure, anticipating sunny days and the corn season. Or I'll do it myself using a steel brush for a moderate structure, or a brass rilling bar for more aggressive and long-lasting rills (lengthwise grooves) in the ski.

If you're on a tour, and forgot to add that structure beforehand, the file from your repair kit—assuming that you have one—can be put up on its edge and drawn lengthwise carefully along the length of the ski to rill the base. Another crude but effective tool is a file card to put rills in the base. Using either a file or file card, use your fingers as guides along the sidewalls of the base to keep your grooves as straight as possible. Use light pressure—it's enough if you see little dents in the base surface. Too much pressure and you'll make grooves that only come out later by seriously grinding the ski.

Check the tips of your skis. Especially if you're free-heel skiing, be sure that your tips aren't too pointy. It may sound improbable, but the suction of very wet snow can stop your skis cold—it's easy to take a "door hinge" fall and get a ski tip in the face.

De-tune the tips and tails. I dull both towards the boot to at least where the ski contacts the snow. You can extend that de-tune up to a foot or so if you're less experienced or you anticipate crusty spring snow.

Photo on following page © Scott Cramer

CONSIDER YOUR BODY POSITION

Some skiers like to lower their center of gravity in slushy snow. Tele skiers, especially, choose a very low telemark in grabby wet conditions. Personally this isn't my first choice. It may be just because I'm not comfortable with it, but for me, getting too low in a tele requires that I shift my body too far forward or back to adjust my weight.

To maintain my balance in grabby snow I prefer my normal stance, which is pretty tall, with my weight shifted slightly rearward. Standing taller I feel that I can adjust quickly back and forth when my skis slow down or speed up.

The key here is that I said *my* normal stance. Experiment with where *you* feel the most comfortable, and go from there. Your sweet spot may be low, mine may be taller. Different body types, types of experience, and types of knee surgeries make different skiers comfortable in very different positions.

EXECUTE SUBTLE TURNS

For stability in wet snow with a lot of suction, you'll need to be subtle in your movements—too much weight on one foot or another will usually decelerate that foot at an alarming rate. I try to make a "sneaky" lead change from tele to tele standing centered *between* my feet. As I change leads, I pull my feet up very slightly, or soften the pressure on my skis, so that there is little resistance as I swap leads. I'm trying to ski very two-footed.

The same thing goes for parallel turns. Ski more two-footed than normal, being very soft on your skis as you change edges, and pressuring both skis rather than just one.

Avoid stepping movements. Stepping pressures the ski that you step off of, and then the ski that you step onto. In stepped turns, it is difficult to anticipate when unpredictable snow will decelerate a pressured ski.

If the snow isn't particularly sucky, just deep and cruddy, you can exaggerate the retraction/extension of your legs to get a good bend and strong turn out of your skis. You might think of it as your powder turn, exaggerated. Some call it a "power turn."

As your skis come across the fall line and you prepare to change your tele lead (or move into a new parallel turn):

- Sink lower than normal.
- Face down the hill, planting your pole to signal a new turn.
- As you change your edges/lead to move into the new turn, extend your feet decisively—even abruptly—to pressure the skis as much as possible at the start of that new arc.

- Extend your feet and steer your skis into the fall line, then sink and steer your skis out of it.

Some skiers prefer to think of it as *standing up* into the new turn, but you aren't really standing up, you're extending your feet and skis into the crud, pressuring your boards into an arc while your body stays quite low to the snow. Think *two-footed* as you extend your feet into your new turn.

Practice these turns one at a time, making each from a traverse while facing down the hill and planting your pole decisively to signal each new extension.

Finally, keep in mind these other little indispensable points.

- Avoid lazy habits when surfing the slush. While slush can be fatiguing, it can also be mushy and forgiving. Stay focused—whatever your favorite focal points are in winter conditions, don't forget them in spring. Facing down the hill, edging (see the next point), flexion and extension of your legs, weight distribution—these are all points to remember in sun-baked slush.
- It is easy to ride a flat ski in slush. Try to keep your skis on edge—flat skis catch outside edges and cause painful slammers in heavy snow. Think "inside corners," "pointing the inside knee," whatever exercises you have to get you up on your edges.
- Use speed prudently. It's tempting to carry a lot of speed in slushy conditions, trying to power through it. This isn't a prudent option in the backcountry, especially with a pack. Remember how quickly your feet can slow down in slushy snow, and ski at a speed where you can adjust for this deceleration rather than launching over the tips.

Try these points when the sun beats down, or on those muggy mornings when it didn't freeze the night before. It's best to think about them one at a time. Find the ones that work best for you and keep them close to mind when the bottom drops out. You might even find yourself looking for sloppy snow, just to put yourself to the test. Of course you can always set your alarm—getting up an hour earlier might save you from the bottomless junk.

Moguls

For years I refused to ski bumps at the resorts. I would go to great lengths to avoid mogul slopes, ricocheting across desperate traverses in search of groomed or windswept terrain. I rationalized that I was a cruiser. The fact was, I wasn't very comfortable in bumps, so I avoided them.

Although it's easy to visualize skiing the steep and deep, I wasn't really good at it back then, especially if it wasn't champagne powder. It wasn't until I learned to ski moguls that the steep and deep got easier. Once armed with better mogul technique, I became less intimidated by those steep shots in the trees. Fall-line turns became the norm, easier to make exactly where I needed to turn. Because I no longer avoided moguls, my favorite ski areas grew acres of new terrain.

You don't need to make lightning tele-lead switches and desperate recoveries to be a good mogul skier. Nor do you need to suffer knee-pounding turns when ricocheting off each mogul. Certain points of focus will help you become a smooth, controlled mogul skier who arrives at the bottom, run after run, with limbs and equipment intact. Many of these moves are the same ones you've focused on all along in your free-heel skiing. They are the same skills, looked at in a slightly bumpier perspective. Since moguls tend to amplify your weaknesses, these on-piste moves can be key to your off-piste performance.

It's most important to make up your mind that moguls aren't the enemy. Gritting your teeth while aggressively slamming each bump won't make them go away. Yeah, people do it under the lifts run after run. They probably have young knees. Skis bend, buckles break, bindings rip out, headaches throb. Stay light and relaxed and flow with the hill and gravity. Don't fight them. Aggressive skiing doesn't just mean heavy and hard; it also means light and quick.

Photo on preceding page
© Mark Shapiro

Something that contributes to that light, quick feeling is *rhythm*. Visit a resort like Telluride or Taos and you'll find many good bump runs—and little else to ski. No doubt there's lots of other terrain, but the long, unbroken steep slopes that characterize these areas are usually well-endowed with moguls. They may look frightening at first, but remember that these noteworthy resorts have bumps shaped by expert skiers. With a relaxed attitude and a little practice you'll find lines through these moguls that are steep but reasonable. Bumps carved with rhythm provide that incredibly exhilarating feeling of weightlessness between turns that is caused by flowing with the pull of gravity.

PRACTICING ON A SMOOTH SLOPE

Let's get on snow. Odd as it sounds, it helps to develop a rhythm for mogul skiing by practicing out of the bumps on a smooth, moderately steep slope. Make a series of short-radius turns, confining them to a narrow imaginary "corridor" down the fall line. Better yet, find a single-width snow-cat track that goes directly downhill and use it for your corridor. If you finish each turn to control your speed you will soon feel the rhythm you're after.

There are a couple of points of focus that I like to use making these short-radius turns. If your rhythm feels jerky and syncopated, think of your poles as the metronome that punctuates each turn. Remember the short-radius pole plants in the chapter Skiing from the Waist Up? Punctuate each turn finish with a determined pole plant, a *sting*, that times your turn and sets your body up for the next turn. In that same section, review "opening the door" and *where* to plant your pole in short-radius turns (see illus. 65).

Try concentrating on facing down the hill even more than you ever have before. How do you face your body down the hill more? Skiers refine their movements in increments. *Facing the fall line* is not the same for a skier working on beginning wedge turns as it is for a skier making advanced parallel turns.

Facing the fall line is crucial in moguls. Look down the hill and feel that light, free separation of your upper and lower body. Your navel should be pointing straight down the fall line. Your torso will "float" down the hill while your skis snap rhythmically back and forth to control your speed. Your abdomen, the connector between that floating torso and those active skis arcing back and forth, will feel like it is getting a workout, flexing and extending.

STARTING IN THE TROUGHS

Most skiers agree it's easiest to begin your mogul skiing in the troughs. Look for a moderately angled mogul slope with small, well-spaced bumps. Good practice bumps are hard to find. Some tips: look for places where bumps are less likely to grow too large—below obstacles like rocks or trees, or on slopes that are occasionally groomed. Ski on the sides of the run, where bumps are usually better spaced, rather than down the middle.

65
To develop a rhythm for mogul skiing, first practice your short-radius turns on a smooth slope

Choose a corridor like the one you used on the smooth slope. Look ahead down the corridor (your *line*) and make those same round, controlled turns in the smooth spots between the moguls (see illus. 66). Stay relaxed, and keep your eyes several bumps ahead. Avoid looking down at your tips—*this is critical*.

The following points will help your mogul skiing. Be sure to think about them *one at a time*. There are a lot of them (see illus. 67).

66
Telemarking in
the troughs

Feet

Converging or diverging skis can be deadly in a sea of bumps. You've got to edge both skis—tele or parallel—to keep them traveling in the same direction. *Edge both skis simultaneously*. Parallel skiers, think about your inside knee: point it in the direction of each new turn. You can actually lead with it. Tele skiers, *edge the rear ski first; initiate the turn with it*. Don't make step-turns; try

67

Teles in moguls: think (one at a time) "feet, shoulders, abdomen, hands, poles, . . ."

initiating each turn with the rear ski. Review the pointy-knee and back-ski points in Advanced Parallel Tips or Advanced Telemark Tips.

Shoulders

If you lean or bank in your turns you might have difficulty getting your skis around. This is a common problem among telemarkers. The symptoms are similar to not facing the fall line: you have good longer turns, but you have difficulty with the short fall-line turns required for moguls. An elegant technique in fast, long-radius turns, banking will only get you into trouble in the bumps.

Think shoulders. Face them down the hill. It may help to actually hold your downhill shoulder back as you plant your pole. This will twist your torso so it faces the fall line, preparing it for the upcoming turn.

Abdomen

As I said before, ski with your abdomen. Point your belly button directly down the hill. Review the string-in-the-navel idea in Skiing from the Waist Up. Feel the muscles on the uphill side of your abdomen stretch, the ones on the downhill side contract. Feel those abdominals doing more of the work.

Hands

Moguls can wreak havoc with a skier's hand position. Uphill hands that persistently drop behind twist the body into the hill and set you up for a nasty fall. Try especially hard to keep your hands down the hill and within your peripheral vision. It helps to think of forcing your uphill hand downhill. It's like punching a bag. Push your uphill hand ahead of the downhill one that's planting the pole.

Poles

As you watch good mogul skiers you will notice the aggressive, determined pole plant that signals each new turn. In short-radius turns through bumps, plant your pole at the finish of each turn to coincide with the *sting* of your edges as you check your speed and set up for the next turn. It's the same thing that we practiced earlier in the corridor.

As important as *when* you plant your pole is *how* and *where*. Plant the basket down the hill beneath your downhill foot so that your body is "open" to the upcoming turn. Reach downhill—not toward your tips. With your skis across the hill, your basket should be back by your heel as you set up for a short-radius turn.

LOG WALKING

An alpine instructor once showed me a trick called "log walking." It works great with either tele or parallel turns. You simply step over the mogul. I know—looking down Tourist Trap at Vail, the idea of stepping over waist-high bumps seems improbable. Trust me. As your ski tips are pushed up by a mogul, step over the top of it with your uphill ski as though the mogul were a log. In a parallel turn step onto your new outside ski and steer it into the fall line. In a telemark, use the bump to slow you as you step over it into your lead change. Tele skiers, *don't forget the rear ski*; come down on *both edges* in your new tele and steer it into the fall line.

Try it. As your skis ride up the bump, quickly step over the top. Alpine skiers will step from one foot to the other—from their current downhill ski to the new outside/downhill ski. Tele skiers will step into a new lead/turn. Exaggerate the movement and you will be log hopping instead of log walking.

It might take more than blithe hopping to get over the tops of huge moguls. You will need more shock absorption with another focus: your knees. I think of *lifting* my knees to absorb an especially large bump. I don't want to wait stiff-legged until the bump shoves my knees up into my chest. It's as though you anticipate each bump in order to soften the blow. Time it right, lift your knees, and you can log walk over even huge bumps.

EXTENDING

Find a skier on the hill who stays low in the bumps. You won't have to look for long because getting low in bumpy situations is a natural reaction. Chances are the skier you're watching will do okay in the first few turns. But he'll soon start getting thrown around and compressed lower and lower until he has nowhere to go. With no more shock absorption he becomes a projectile ricocheting off each undulation in the terrain. Stuck in the back seat, he's lost his shock absorption by overcompressing his springs—his legs. By *extending your legs* between turns and standing tall, you can stretch those springs to prepare for another compression.

That's the other half of that leg-lifting business: *extending your legs*. Log walking helps because there's a natural extension when you step over something. But if you feel as though you are getting smaller and smaller as you pound down the hill, try extending your legs as you press your skis "into the valley" once you step over the bump. You might think of it as standing up, although it's much more of a leg extension movement than truly standing up.

If you are turning in the troughs, the motion will be the same as in skiing deep snow, when you press your skis into a new turn as you drop off your platform. Using parallels, rise over the mogul, press on the balls of your feet, and press your tips down into the trough. In a telemark, keep plenty of weight on that back ski and edge as you press the front ski into the trough. In either turn, you will feel as though your legs are shock absorbers, compressing to absorb the high spots, storing energy, then springing back and extending into the low spots.

Try this exercise: take a shallow traverse across a mogul slope, no turns, absorbing the moguls by pulling up on your knees and then extending your feet into the troughs. Try to *keep your head the same height*. Do the absorbing with your knees and ankles, and keep your head the same height as you traverse the slope.

I find that this "head height" exercise is an especially important one for telemark skiers. Most tele skiers have trained themselves in the telemark lead change to stand up as they change leads. In this exercise, try changing leads as you go over the bumps *without standing up*. You'll need to consciously pull up on your feet so that instead of standing up during this lead change, you absorb the bump. I think of pulling up on my knees, sneaking my front foot back and back foot forward in the lead change. As you extend down the other side, instead of standing up, think of letting your *legs get longer*. I know—it's an esoteric idea until you get into moguls or uneven terrain; but it's possible to think of the head being level and, rather than compressing your whole body and then "standing up," think of the legs *coming up* to go over a bump, then *extending* into the next low spot.

I think of pulling my legs up under me, then pushing my feet into the trough. For me, even better than thinking of keeping my head level is thinking of keeping my *navel* level. Try it: in your bump traverse, flex and extend your legs, keeping your *navel* at the same level (refer back to illus. 67).

Once you feel your body is "quieter" and your legs are doing the absorption work in this vertical plane, see if you can feel them getting more out to the side in your turns and then coming under you between turns. That's the ultimate step for rounder turns in the bumps. Refer to "Crossover" in the chapter Skiing from the Waist Up for more on this idea.

Each day you venture into the bumps you will find yourself more in tune with your body's position and less intimidated by surprises. You will begin to venture into the bumps purposefully—or at least not go out of your way to avoid them. Your favorite ski area will get bigger, the backcountry easier. Your skiing will improve—even on the steep and deep!

Jordi

~

Down from the Haute Route, we sipped a beer in the Zermatt Bahnhofstübe with our Andorran acquaintances from the tour. Andorra is a tiny principality trapped in a mountain cirque between France and Spain. Although they carry French passports, the Andorrans seemed much more like gregarious Spanish or Italians than brooding French. Among their group of five they seemed to speak just about everything: Catalan, their local dialect, and its cousin, Spanish; French, because they carry French passports and work with the French; English, to speak to the tight-fisted Brits who frequent their duty-free country; and Italian because . . . why not? It's the best food.

The rowdy Andorrans had just finished the route and were waiting to catch a train. Jordi, the star, was beyond euphoria. A mid-thigh amputee, Jordi had just completed Chamonix–Zermatt on his only leg. He used one ski and outriggers. As far as his friends knew he was the first.

I looked at Jordi and thought back to that long, hot day from Mont Fort (Verbier) to the Cabane du Dix. Four passes. A 4:00 A.M.

start with headlamps. Noisy skiing on a rock-hard crust with full hardware: heel lifters, skins, and *harscheisen* (ski crampons). We climbed Rosablanche, dropped into a short, steep couloir to long, perfect corn slopes and the Lac du Dix. The long traverse around Dix was a significant thrash over kilometers of avalanche debris. The last climb was a sweltering slog up 3000 feet to the Dix hut. All afternoon we lolled outdoors rehydrating, alternately taking sun and trying to get out of it. A typical randonnée afternoon, it was too soft to ski. We dozed, lazy in the warm light and cool breeze of the huge cirque, woozy from the tasteless, priceless French beer.

Lolling away, we knew that Jordi was below us, poling across the debris. He and his friends arrived during dinner. The entire hut (more than a hundred people) evacuated the dining room and cheered him up the final steep slope. Most of us had just done the same tour, on two legs, and we were trashed. Jordi swung up the last step, twisted out of his ski, and collapsed into a seat on the porch. He was still smiling and good-natured. "*Sono distrutto*," he told me in Italian. "I am destroyed."

The next day he got up early and did it again.

The shorter days were better as one could get off of the snow before it became too soft. For Jordi, on firmer frozen corn, his cramponed outriggers gave great purchase. He had quite a system for climbing: a skin and ski crampon for the ski, and outriggers with crampons that were (tediously) screwed onto their little skis for each climb. For each uphill step he first placed the outriggers' crampons, leaned on them, and swung his leg through. On steep climbs that required step-kicking he carried his ski, used the outriggers like semi-horizontal handrails, and did a dip up on those handrails to gain altitude. A friend in front prepared the steps, a friend in back helped place his foot in difficult spots. Some of these difficult spots had thousands of feet of exposure. Each descent required that Jordi's "engineer" friend remove the screwed-on crampons to expose the outriggers' skis. When he got his spikes off and started down, the guy flew like a bird.

On the downhill, Jordi was one of the best skiers of the lot, especially in the worst snow. He never seemed to need his outriggers, carving his single ski elegantly through the crustiest conditions. He was so accomplished with this system that I wondered if he had always skied on one leg. After one descent, looking back on his beautiful arcs, he told me his story. At a ski area in Andorra, in thick fog, he had struck a snow cat that was preparing a slope. He lost his smashed leg. He was seventeen when he had his accident; this trip was its tenth anniversary. He had always wanted to do the Haute Route.

© Paul Parker

Bibliography

Abraham, Horst. *Skiing Right.* Boulder, Colorado: Johnson Books, 1983.

Hall, Bill. *Cross-Country Skiing Right.* San Francisco: Harper and Row, 1985.

Joubert, Georges. *Teaching Yourself to Ski.* Aspen, Colorado: Aspen Ski Masters, 1970.

Lunn, Arnold. *A History of Skiing.* Oxford: Oxford University Press, 1927.

Tejada-Flores, Lito. *Backcountry Skiing: The Sierra Club Guide to Skiing off the Beaten Track.* San Francisco: Sierra Club Books, 1981.

Tejada-Flores, Lito. *Breakthrough on Skis: How to Get Out of the Intermediate Rut.* New York: Vintage Books, 1986.

Witherell, Warren, and David Evrard. *The Athletic Skier.* Salt Lake City: The Athletic Skier, Inc., 1993.

Index

About the Author

Paul Parker has been telemark skiing for over thirty years. He is a certified ski instructor in both nordic and alpine skiing, and a former member of the Professional Ski Instructors of America's Nordic Demonstration Team. Involved for many years in developing new products for telemark, including boot and ski design, he currently develops skis for Tua Ski and boots and outerwear for Garmont. He lives in Breckenridge, Colorado.

© Brian Litz